Praise for Denise Duffield-Thomas

*'Denise Duffield-Thomas [is] one of the foremost
financial advisors for females.'*
ENTREPRENEUR.COM

*'Denise Duffield-Thomas is a much-needed voice of practical
wisdom for women looking to build a financially thriving future.
She's also a shining example of what it means to create a
business and life you love while also serving the world.'*
MARIE FORLEO, FOUNDER OF MARIETV, B-SCHOOL, AND MARIEFORLEO.COM

*'Denise has helped her growing community of 120,000+ business
owners overcome their money blocks and build successful companies.'*
FORBES.COM

*'Denise is one of the most honest, transparent, unapologetic voices
out there leading women to prosperity. Her work is so important.'*
KATE NORTHRUP, AUTHOR OF *MONEY, A LOVE STORY*

*'Denise offers ... so much value and openly and honestly shares
what has worked well for her business – and what has not.'*
HUFFPOST

*'Every single one of us has the ability to create so much success,
and what I love about Denise is her ability to show people the
way. She's empowered so many women to create the business
and life they dreamed of – everyone needs to listen up.'*
CARRIE GREEN, FOUNDER OF THE FEMALE ENTREPRENEUR
ASSOCIATION AND AUTHOR OF *SHE MEANS BUSINESS*

*'What I love about Denise is her ability to demonstrate that it
doesn't have to be all about hustle and grind!* Chillpreneur *shows
that you can make money doing what you love and take great care
of yourself and your family along the way, without the stress or
burnout. Her authenticity and expertise has inspired me since the very
beginning of my journey into business, mindset, and abundance.'*
MEL WELLS, AUTHOR OF *THE GODDESS REVOLUTIO'* *HUNGRY FOR MORE*

'In a world that traditionally celebrates "busy" as a badge of honor, Denise is leading the way with a fresh (and much-needed) approach to entrepreneurship. With easy-to-follow steps and her signature down-to-earth style, we can all put our feet up and breathe a sigh of relief that running our own business no longer has to lead to burnout.'

AMANDA JANE DALEY, BUSINESS MENTOR TO WELLNESS ENTREPRENEURS

'Chillpreneur is a much-needed antidote to today's busy-worshipping culture, and a complete breath of fresh air for over-hustled women in business everywhere. In true Denise style, this book is full of no-BS, practical advice for creating success without the stress.'

KATE MCKIBBIN, FUNNEL AND MARKETING MENTOR

'Denise's approach to business is smart, funny, HONEST, and delightfully practical. In her books, her programs, her LIFE... she's walking her Chillpreneur talk, holding up the mirror to remind us that when in doubt (or stuck in overwhelm, perfectionism, or shoulds), "there are easier ways to make money."'

NIKKI ELLEDGE BROWN, AUTHOR AND CREATOR OF A COURSE ABOUT COPY® AND NAPTIME EMPIRES™

'Chillpreneur almost sounds too good to be true, especially living in a world where the word "hustle" seems like the only prescription for a successful business. Denise offers an alternative that intersects intentional manifesting and mindful actions which keeps you and your business in receiving mode, while giving you more energy, time, and money as you grow in your entrepreneurship'

JENNIFER KEM, FOUNDER OF THE MASTER BRAND METHOD

'Denise and I are so on the same page when it comes to designing your business around what you love most. Chillpreneur makes it crystal clear that you simply don't need to overcomplicate anything. By being a Chillpreneur you commit to simplifying everything, focusing on your strengths, appreciating what you already have, and then sitting back to watch the abundance and joy you've manifested into your life as a result! In a world where too many people are stressed out, burned out, anxious, and hustling like crazy, Denise's book is a breath of fresh air to do the exact opposite. It's a must read!'

NATALIE SISSON, FREEDOMIST AND AUTHOR OF THE FREEDOM PLAN AND THE SUITCASE ENTREPRENEUR

Chillpreneur

Also by Denise Duffield-Thomas

*Lucky Bitch: A Guide for Exceptional Women
to Create Outrageous Success*

*Get Rich, Lucky Bitch!: Release Your Money
Blocks and Live a First-Class Life*

Chillpreneur

The New Rules for Creating Success, Freedom, and Abundance on Your Terms

DENISE DUFFIELD-THOMAS

HAY HOUSE

Carlsbad, California • New York City
London • Sydney • New Delhi

Published in the United Kingdom by:
Hay House UK Ltd, The Sixth Floor, Watson House
54 Baker Street, London W1U 7BU
Tel: +44 (0)20 3927 7290; Fax: +44 (0)20 3927 7291; www.hayhouse.co.uk

Published in the United States of America by:
Hay House Inc., PO Box 5100, Carlsbad, CA 92018-5100
Tel: (1) 760 431 7695 or (800) 654 5126; Fax: (1) 760 431 6948 or (800) 650 5115
www.hayhouse.com

Published in Australia by:
Hay House Australia Ltd, 18/36 Ralph St, Alexandria NSW 2015
Tel: (61) 2 9669 4299; Fax: (61) 2 9669 4144; www.hayhouse.com.au

Published in India by:
Hay House Publishers India, Muskaan Complex, Plot No.3, B-2,
Vasant Kunj, New Delhi 110 070
Tel: (91) 11 4176 1620; Fax: (91) 11 4176 1630; www.hayhouse.co.in

A catalogue record for this book is available from the British Library.

Tradepaper ISBN: 978-1-4019-6062-9
E-book ISBN: 978-1-78817-140-3
Audiobook ISBN: 978-1-78817-338-4

Interior images: 1, 55, 123, 195: Fotolia; author photo 273: Claire Thomasina J;
all other images: Shutterstock

Printed in the United States of America

11 10 9 8 7 6 5 4 3

This book is dedicated to my family.
Thanks for supporting my work
(even on my not-so-chilled days)
so that together, we can create a life of
freedom, adventure, abundance, and JOY.

Contents

Introduction

You've heard of resting bitch face, right? Well, apparently, I have resting chill face. Everyone assumes that I'm calm, collected, and never stressed about anything. 'Denise, you're so *relaxed!*' they say. 'What's your secret?'

Maybe it's because I'm Australian: as a nation, we're notoriously laid-back, and our unofficial motto is: 'She'll be right, mate.' But the truth is, I wasn't born with a happy-go-lucky personality: I've *consciously* learned how to cultivate that attitude. Remember the book *Don't Sweat the Small Stuff... and It's All Small Stuff?* Well, I used to sweat *everything*. Literally. Anxiety often made me a sweaty, stinky mess. And then I'd get worried about *that* too.

In my early days as an employee and a fledgling entrepreneur, I was riddled with insecurity. I worried about everything, but especially about making mistakes. I second-guessed every word I spoke or wrote, and constantly thought:

- ✦ Am I good enough to make it?

- ✦ Was that really a good session with my client? Or is she regretting working with me? She'll probably ask for a refund, won't she?

❖ Did I say that in the right tone of voice? Did I apologize too much? Was I too demanding?

I was terrified of opening my email inbox because I was sure I'd find bad news, like a complaint, a refund request, or hate mail. In snail mail, I just expected bills, parking fines, or speeding tickets. I was afraid of getting things wrong, like which system to use, which book to write first (I've always had a million ideas floating around my head), or whether a specific coach was right for me. I was in analysis paralysis because I second-guessed myself at every turn, and the consequences of making the wrong decision seemed catastrophic.

I even worried about what would happen if I *did* become wildly successful. I had a recurring nightmare about being a regular on Oprah's show and having to wake up at 4:30 a.m. every day for hair and makeup. I'd lie awake and stress: 'But I like my sleep! How do I say no to *Oprah*?' I barely had a business, but I had tons of worries about it!

Personal development helped a lot. Through it all, I had an underlying belief that, one day, I would be successful, even though I was so often anxious. I always had big dreams and just knew I'd be a millionaire one day.

I always wanted to run my own business. Even as a kid, I was the 'go-to' girl for others. I had a knack for breaking down people's problems and helping them, even if all I did was reassure them that, somehow, we'd figure it out together. When my friends' parents thought I was dealing drugs to their teenagers, I was just selling self-help! 'Don't worry, let's journal it out,' I'd tell my friends. Or I'd parrot Oprah advice I'd heard on TV.

My academic advisor at university laughed at my A+ grades in marketing and my Fs in economics, statistics, and accounting. 'Denise, you're so creative, but your assignments are full of BS,' he said. 'In 10 years' time, you'll either be a millionaire or in jail for fraud.' Well, here I am, free as a bird, a self-made millionaire using my powers for good! Rather than learning to be a better statistician or economist, I doubled down on my creativity and became an entrepreneur!

When I started teaching my first personal development workshops (at age 19), I was surprised that people listened to what I had to say. Even though I was just regurgitating the words of the male self-help gurus of the time, people *believed* in the borrowed confidence that helped me believe in myself.

Slowly, slowly, I got more traction in my business, until I became one of those 20-years-in-the-making 'overnight successes' and could legitimately call myself a millionaire. Along the way, I got more chill about making mistakes (I still make them all the time), and I stopped caring (as much) about whether everyone liked me. I finally learned not to sweat the proverbial small stuff.

The idea of being a Type A personality never quite resonated with me – although I'm hardworking and ambitious, I've never been about winning for the sake of winning. I'm not really competitive, even though I have high standards for myself; Type B seemed more my style. But I realized there's a third category that's even more my style: Type C – a chilled, ambitious-but-lazy, wants-to-change-the-world-but-also-thinks-there's-an-easier-way person.

That's what this book is about. I'm not going to teach you how to hustle or tell you to get up earlier (the older I get, the more I realize how important sleep is). I'm actually going to teach you the opposite – business really doesn't have to be that hard! You can get to a place where your business supports your dreams but doesn't burn you out. Where you feel 'enoughness' at the end of the day, but you're excited to achieve your next big goal.

There's never been a better time to be a woman in business, and the opportunities before us are mind-blowing. Freedom and independence can be yours with just a little bit of upfront work. I don't understand, technically, how the internet works, but the tools we have available to us are magical and life-changing.

When I count my blessings and write my gratitude list, you'd better believe that techy geeks are on it, because they helped me change my life, and in turn, the lives of thousands of other women. All hail those Silicon Valley dudes (let's face it, most of them are men). They might not be the most feminist people, but they've created opportunities for women like us to gain an unprecedented level of economic independence, and for that, I'm grateful.

Being an entrepreneur once required a lot of upfront capital for machines and stock, or techy know-how. It felt official and serious, like a title that was bestowed upon you (maybe even by a business school). An entrepreneur was either a crazy inventor or a door-to-door salesman. You were restricted by where you lived, so too bad if that was some crappy little town in the middle of nowhere.

Hey, but not now! Today, anyone can start a business, good or bad. As long as you have internet access, you can sell glitter penis-grams from your tiny house in Nebraska. You can design websites from the beach in Tulum, Mexico. Or you can run a global coaching business from a small town in Australia (even with crappy internet), which is exactly how I got started.

There's no limit to what you can do. Not everyone will succeed the first (or 40th) time, but while failure used to mean bankruptcy or piles of unwanted stuff in your garage, now you can just close up your (Etsy) shop and try something else. No big deal: there are plenty more ideas in the sea! Women are succeeding more than ever and are finally seeing entrepreneurship as a viable vehicle for supporting their families, for creating wealth for themselves and others, and for changing the world.

But it's not all sunshine and roses. Even though women (especially women of color) are the fastest-growing group of entrepreneurs, we come with a lot of built-in obstacles. Being an entrepreneur used to mean men in suits, and now it's bro-dudes in hoodies. Women's businesses aren't always considered 'real enterprises' or respected by mainstream entrepreneurial publications. There's a very real wage gap in the entrepreneurial world, too. But nobody can work harder than a woman with a dream, and most women I meet are *more than* smart and creative enough. The biggest problem is that we're still trying to fit our businesses into an old, masculine model. And that's exhausting!

What Inspired This Book?

I love business books, but at some point, I noticed the usual ones stopped resonating with me. So much so that one day, I briefly considered throwing the book I was reading across the room. I may even have sworn at it.

It was a bestselling title about how world-class performers live and work, and the case study I'd just read featured a 'successful' entrepreneur who got up every day at 4:30 a.m. to work on his blog, went to the gym at 8 a.m., then headed to the office, where he worked until 6:30 p.m. After that, he went home, had dinner, and spent an hour with his wife and child; he then worked again from 9 p.m. until 1 a.m., slept on the couch, and woke the next morning to do it all again – on three hours' sleep.

I actually wrote 'WTF!' in the margin. My first thought was, *He has a* kid*? And a* wife*?* My second thought was, *Wait.* This *is success?* These business books were full of talk about 'crushing your goals' and 'killing your competition.' It was the old, patriarchal nonsense that still permeates entrepreneurial culture.

> *'I am endlessly fascinated that playing football is considered a training ground for leadership, but raising children isn't.'*
>
> DEE DEE MYERS

But at the beginning of my business, I didn't know any better. I regularly woke at 4:30 a.m. to work with international clients. I worked day and night. I dreamed about clients and spreadsheets in my sleep. I never had time for friends, let alone decent meals. I was obsessed with 'making it' at all costs, and it wasn't healthy.

Everyone's version of success is different, but most of the women I talk with these days have lost a certain amount of *richness* in their lives. They feel like they're working harder than ever for diminishing returns, both in a financial sense and in satisfaction with their work. They are missing the *joy*.

Hustling for cash is exhausting. Most of us are juggling our business dreams with partners, kids, family obligations, school, waxing appointments, and just *life*. You don't want to work all day and night. You want time to go to the beach, get to that yoga class, see your friends and family, and be a more present partner, mother, sister, and friend. And you can. But it's really common to get sucked into the trap of: 'If I want more money, I have to work *harder.*' Most of the methods we use in our work, and the books we read, have been created and governed by masculine models of success. I never questioned that until I burned myself out.

> *'Entrepreneurs are the only people who will work 80 hours a week to avoid working 40 hours a week for someone else.'*
>
> LORI GREINER

Why was I waking up at 4:30 a.m. when I started my business? Well, I had clients on the other side of the world, and I felt bad about asking them to work with me outside their normal hours. (Oh boy, we're going to have an honest conversation about boundaries later in this book.) Why did I often pull all-nighters? I once worked on a sales page all night, followed by three straight hours of coaching calls, and then delivered a live webinar – all on no sleep. I did this because I felt terrible about the idea of hiring someone and asking for help. If you suck at this, too, don't worry: I have some tips for you later.

Back then, my friend James Wedmore told me, 'Denise, you can't get to six figures by doing it all yourself.' My answer? 'Watch me.' Yeah, that's stupid. But when I *did* hit six figures, I felt a massive wave of discouragement instead of celebration. I was a 'success story,' but not really. My success didn't feel sustainable (in truth, it felt like a massive fluke), and there was no obvious way to increase my income without working harder. I was already stressed and tired.

In my early days in business, I met a fellow coach who told me she saw 100 clients a week. My first thought was, *When do you pee?* My second was, *Oh my God – I energetically max out at 15 clients a week.* I probably made the same amount of money as she did, and I instantly felt guilty for working fewer hours than I 'should.' *Maybe I should see 100 clients?* I thought. *What's wrong with me?*

I honestly believed that taking any shortcut was lazy, instead of smart. But the truth is that we've all started our business for the freedom and flexibility it gives us, not to replicate our old jobs, and definitely not to do *more* work for less lifestyle. I wanted a business that helped others, was wildly profitable, but didn't suck all my energy and time or leave me a husk of a person attached to my computer screen. It was time for a new breed of entrepreneur. It was time for the Chillpreneur.

I know, I know. Everyone is some type of '-preneur' these days; it's *beyond* cheesy. But most of the heart-centered women I know don't want to hustle anymore. We don't want to 'crush' anything, especially not the competition. We want to *collaborate* with other women, not *kill* them! We want *everyone* to succeed. And we'd also love to have the time to create a garden, have a hobby, or get our hair and nails done occasionally.

Is that too much to ask? No.

As you'll discover in this book, being a Chillpreneur isn't about swinging around in a hammock all day long (I've been in a hammock twice in my life, and I fell out of it the first time) or living in Bali (though you can be a Chillpreneur there, too). It's about finding a new way of doing business: one that works for your bank account *and* supports your wellbeing; one that works for you *and* the planet; and one that follows the path of least resistance.

Hear this from a recovering perfectionist workaholic who is now a pretty chilled-out millionaire with young kids: it's possible, and this book will show you how.

What Is a Chillpreneur?

> *'My guiding principle is that prosperity can be shared. We can create wealth together. The global economy is not a zero-sum game.'*
>
> JULIA GILLARD, FORMER PRIME MINISTER OF AUSTRALIA

I have seven suggestions for becoming a Chillpreneur. I sincerely wish I was perfect at all seven of these, but they're aspirational even for me. Take what's useful and leave what isn't – this is about finding *your* path of least resistance.

1. You Believe in a Benevolent Universe – for Everyone

As a Chillpreneur, you embrace an abundant mindset and accept that there's enough for everyone, including money, clients, and opportunities. You know you're just as deserving as anyone else, and that your gain isn't someone else's loss.

2. You Embrace Your Humanity

Being chill doesn't mean you have to be zen all the time or nun-like in your approach to life. As a Chillpreneur, you're perfectly imperfect just the way you are. You're going to have days when you're decidedly *unchill* about everything, but you practice self-compassion and self-forgiveness for your all-too-human mistakes.

3. You Practice Optimism

As a Chillpreneur, you see the silver lining in everything. Failed launch? 'We can learn *so* much from this for next time!' Tech screw-up in the middle of a webinar? 'Sweet, this is a juicy chapter for my next book!' Everything is useful, and nothing is wasted. In fact, failures are great fodder for podcasts, blog posts, and future Oprah interviews.

4. You Care, But Are Detached from the Outcome

As a Chillpreneur, you know that a client's 'no' doesn't mean you're terrible at your business. Setbacks just mean you need to try again. You genuinely and passionately care about your work, but you still hold it lightly, including your reaction to sales numbers, client results, and feedback from others. Your emotional equilibrium is steady, regardless of what's happening on the outside. You practice self-acceptance rather than being buffeted by others' changing opinions.

5. You Aren't Dogmatic

Chillpreneurs know there are many paths to success. Why spend years debating which way to go when you can just get started on your journey? You're not rigid or stubborn in your thinking and you learn from your mistakes. As a Chillpreneur, you know that imperfect action is better than inaction. You trust that you'll make the best decision for now and tweak as you go.

6. You Follow the Path of Least Resistance

As a Chillpreneur, you don't over-complicate things for the sake of complexity. You don't reinvent the wheel to create more work so you can justify your success to others. You try to find the most comfortable path, even when it feels lazy or too obvious – to yourself or others. You know that ease and flow are different for everyone, so you honor your strengths and weaknesses and don't copy someone else's version of success.

7. You're Driven By a Desire to Do Good in the World

Chillpreneurs strive for mutual success. As a Chillpreneur, you don't think that making money is evil because you know it enables you to do tremendous good in the world. You build philanthropy, self-care, and sustainable practices into your business for the sake of your clients, your team, yourself, and the planet. You're in business to make a lot of money *and* help a lot of people. You know you're one of the good guys.

That's my definition of a Chillpreneur, and you might now be thinking, *Um, that's a* lot *to live up to!* But as I said, I'm not there yet myself – not every day, at least. That's why these are *suggestions*, not commandments. These are the things that I – and many women in my community – strive to create: chilled-out ease, flow, and sustainable success. Being a Chillpreneur is a practice. I'm still in my 'chillprenticeship,' so I'm no Jedi master. Even though I've found my path, I still have to practice this stuff every day.

It's perfect that I started writing this book during one of the hardest years of my entrepreneurial journey. I temporarily forgot that life is allowed to be easy and that you don't have to put literal blood, sweat, and tears (ew) into your business. I forgot that you don't have to sacrifice your adrenals, your marriage, or your sleep to create success in your life. I'll tell you about the mistakes I've made, so you can see how easy it is to fall back into old habits if you're not vigilant. Plus, I want to show you that perfection isn't the end game. Through reading about my errors, big and small, you can avoid the same pitfalls.

A key part of creating a Chillpreneur lifestyle is learning how to work less and earn more. Can we really create a business that works for us in every way, bringing joy *and* cash? This book aims to answer that question in the most practical ways possible. We're going to work on your mindset, but also on how to bring in actual money, so you can pay for real-world stuff like ballet lessons, the mortgage, and maybe a few more crystals for your collection!

You'll be inspired to use your business as a catalyst for manifesting big goals, like buying your dream house, traveling the world, becoming a philanthropist, even becoming a millionaire if you want to. And through everything, I will inspire you to find your path of least resistance. That's my guiding mantra: *path of least resistance*.

How to Read This Book 'Perfectly'

Do you want to know how to *crush* this book and *win* at reading it? Yeah… no. There's no badge for finishing it in record time, and no prizes for perfection. There are five parts to the book:

✦ **Mindset** (getting your head on straight)

✦ **Business Models** (how to structure your business for success)

✦ **Money** (how to make it, ask for it, and protect it)

✦ **Marketing** (how to get clients)

✦ **Your Mission** (a call to action)

Although each part builds on and references the one before it, you can read the parts in any order – choose-your-own-adventure style. Feel free to dip in and out of the book when you feel like you need some advice or a shot of motivation.

I highly recommend you use a journal while reading this book, but I've created a bonus online 'Action Guide' that summarizes the main points of each chapter and has all the exercises in one handy place.

It's perfect if you want to revisit the key concepts but don't have time to reread the book from cover to cover. Download it at Chillpreneur.com/Bonus (do this now, before you forget).

Before we move on to the first chapter, let's take a deep breath and say my favorite mantra together: '*It's my time, and I'm ready for the next step.*' I can show you the path, but you have to decide on your own that you're ready to walk it. You won't have to make big, dramatic changes, just take a teeny baby step forward and the next action will become clear. Someone has already invented every conceivable tool you'll need to support your business (and think how many more are to come!) Your ideas might not yet be fully formed, but you have everything you need to birth them.

The time is now. You're ready.

If there's one thing I want you to remember from this book, it's that *you are enough*. You don't need anything in particular to be successful, and there's no height or weight requirement for wealth. Your accent is beautiful as it is. Your hair is perfect. Your age right now is the right age to start.

Why not you? Why not us? Why not now?

You might not *feel* ready, and that's okay. Because it *is* your time, and together we'll figure it out as we go along. Ready to embrace the Chillpreneur lifestyle? I promise it will be fun and profitable!

— PART I —

Mindset

Chapter 1

Playing the Game of Business

*'Most people consider life a battle, but
it is not a battle, it is a game.'*

Florence Scovel Shinn

*H*aving created a multimillion-dollar business without taking
outside investment or working my guts out (while also raising
young kids), many women ask me my number-one secret to success.
The answer is: *mindset*. Constantly working on your mindset is
honestly the most important – if not the only – thing you have to
master. Everything else, you can just Google. Really. Business isn't
that complicated.

Unfortunately, women often think they need more qualifications,
a new funnel, or a different website, instead of working on their fears,
beliefs, and other mindset issues. (Seriously, stop worrying about
your funnels, you'll figure it out.) Of course, you need a product or
service that people want to buy, you need to market yourself, and

there are a million logistical things to do, but without the right mindset, everything else will fall apart.

And many women also think they have to be perfect before they can start: an attitude that's the antithesis of being a Chillpreneur – it will derail you and make things way harder than they need to be.

Basically, being in business is like playing a giant, real-life game of snakes and ladders (aka chutes and ladders). The board-game version is a game of chance. If you roll the dice and happen to land on a snake (chute), you fall behind. Bad luck. And if you land on a ladder, you get to skip ahead. There's no skill involved at all – your fortune is totally determined by the luck of the dice.

In reality, I believe we make our own luck. In the world of entrepreneurship, each time you encounter an obstacle, you can choose how you engage with it. You can't avoid obstacles, but fortunately, you don't need to do that to 'win' the game. The weird thing is that, when normal, inevitable challenges come up – like a refund request – some people not only fall down, they launch themselves down a snake/chute and refuse to play the game again, convinced they're a failure. They quit, or remain paralyzed by fear, shame, and indecision for years.

Knowing ahead of time about these inevitable rites of passage gives you the opportunity to be reasonably chill about things you can't avoid. It's unlikely that you'll have zero refund requests for your services; so if you know that they're inevitable, you can stop 'pre-worrying' about them, and they won't bother you as much when they happen (and they will).

You have a choice: throw yourself down a snake/chute and stop playing the game, or shrug, pick yourself up, and roll the dice to see what's next in your entrepreneurial adventure. Being an entrepreneur isn't life-or-death. In the grand scheme of things, it's not that serious or hard. As scary as it is some days, it's still better than doing a job you hate or wasting your potential.

I'm not that amazing at business, but I know how to play the game. I've become successful because I choose to see obstacles as inevitable rites of passage along the path to my destiny. I've experienced the same challenges as any other entrepreneur, but I've always found a way to reframe them instead of letting them derail me.

Seriously, I've celebrated every 'bad' thing that has happened because I know it brings me one step closer to success. My first one-star book review on Amazon? I celebrated! My first refund request? I felt like I'd made it! It's not that these things felt good (far from it): I just knew that it was a mark of success, like making it through to the next level of a challenging video game. I made it through and I didn't die! Whoo-hoo! See the difference?

How many people do you know who have experienced an ordinary setback like this and just quit in shame and fear? I've seen women quit after a single refund request, convinced they must be terrible at their business. I've seen women give up after a less-than-spectacular launch, not realizing that anyone who has created a thriving business had crappy launches too.

Everyone starts from zero, *everyone*! The journey is inescapable. You have to be willing to get through everything on your way to your fabulous life. Playing the game doesn't mean you won't get scared. In fact, the biggest obstacle you'll face is fear.

Do You Really Have What It Takes?

You might be thinking *I'm not brave enough to do this*. Or *I'm not competitive enough to make it in business*. I understand. I don't even like playing Monopoly, and I'm not at all cutthroat. Plus, I'm the biggest introvert in the world. But the belief that you have to be a certain way or a particular personality type comes from a place of scarcity. There's more than enough business to go around, but we've been taught from a young age that there are only a few slots available for success, and they go to the most competitive, deserving, or ambitious.

I call this the 'Highlander Myth.' *Highlander* is a cult 1986 movie starring Christopher Lambert and Sean Connery whose premise is that some immortal Highlander warriors have to defeat each other for the ultimate prize: the power to rule the world. There's no amicable sharing of power. It's a fight to the death, and the winner absorbs the other's life-force after basically decapitating him for no reason other than to win. On its release, the movie's tagline was 'There can be only One.'

I don't know about you, but I don't want to rule the world: I just want to contribute to making it a better place. I don't want to kill my competitors – I actually like them. I'm just not that competitive or ruthless; I want everyone to win! Before you beat yourself up for not having the right 'edge' to make it in business, think about the messages you've been absorbing your whole life: success is a zero-sum game. This age-old story leads to all sorts of screwed-up business beliefs, including:

❖ There can be only one person like me in my industry or niche.

❖ There's only one guru of the gurus.

❖ There can be only one success story in my peer group.

How many times have you come up with a great idea, but thought it was already taken? Or believed you have to be the Oprah of your industry, and therefore didn't even try? Think of the 'cool girl' in your industry. Do you compare yourself (unfavorably) to her? Is she your benchmark of success because she seems to be the popular one who everyone wants to work with?

Good news: you don't have to decapitate her to be successful in business! Whew, right? She's probably no more special than you are; there's room for you, too. You just have to release some of your old programming about competition. There's only one Oprah, and there's only one you. You have just as much right to be here as anyone else. So, every time you think you're not unique enough to make it, remember: you don't have to kill everyone else in your industry and absorb their power. There's more than enough to go around!

It's not just *Highlander*. Pretty much every movie perpetuates this 'there can be only one' myth, especially when there's room for only one primary female character. She's usually of royal birth (Princess Leia, Snow White, Wonder Woman), The Smart One (Hermione Granger), or the token minority character (where there's definitely only one).

Back in 1991, Katha Pollitt of *New York* magazine coined a term for these token female characters: the 'Smurfette Principle.' She says: 'The message is clear. Boys are the norm, girls the variation; boys are central; girls peripheral; boys are individuals, girls types. Boys define the group, its story and its code of values. Girls exist only in relation to boys.'[1]

In the Smurfs cartoon, there was Brainy Smurf, Clumsy Smurf, Greedy Smurf, Hefty Smurf, Jokey Smurf, and... Vagina Smurf. Sorry, I mean Smurfette: the only female Smurf in the whole village. Smurfette didn't have any defining attributes or personality traits – she was special because she was the Only.

But that's the message all around us. Most reality shows follow the same concept: there can be only one winner. Participants have to compete and be eliminated each week until there's only one contestant left. Most of the time, there isn't even a prize for the runner-up! Everyone else must lose, which sucks, because most women don't want to win at the expense of someone else. It feels mean and bitchy, especially if you've ever been excluded from the 'cool group' yourself.

Choosing Yourself

The great news is that you don't have to be the best or the smartest to succeed in business. It's not a popularity contest, and there's more than enough room for everyone. *But you do have to choose yourself.*

And that's one of the hardest mindset lessons to master: I deserve success. I'm good enough. I'm ready. I believe in myself.

It feels presumptuous to choose yourself. Women, especially, aren't supposed to brag or be too confident. It feels audacious to say that you like and believe in yourself, let alone believe in your business success.

> *'I had to make my own living and my own opportunity!*
> *But I made it! Don't sit down and wait for the*
> *opportunities to come. Get up and make them.'*
> MADAM C.J. WALKER

I once had a dude at a barbecue ask my husband how my business was doing, and when Mark said, 'Great, actually!' the guy responded, 'Well, some people will buy any old shit, won't they?' I couldn't believe it! Obviously if I was successful without working hard, I must be somehow scamming people.

Sometimes I forget that my business success isn't the norm. I chose myself. I self-published my first books, built my first website myself, and had the audacity to run my own workshops before anyone else thought I was worthy enough. No way was I going to wait until the dice rolled a lucky number. I decided I was enough to get started and to build success, despite what other people thought.

Here's the thing: nobody is going to give you permission to be successful, so stop waiting for external validation. I know – waiting for someone to pick you can be excruciating. Remember at school when you had to line up and wait for the team captains to pick those they wanted on their side? It can feel that way in business, too – like someone else has to deem you ready for the big stage.

The truth is that you'll never feel ready enough, and chances are that nobody is going to 'choose' you. You have to choose yourself. When I first started teaching personal development, I didn't exactly look and feel like a success story, especially when I drove up in my dodgy 20-year-old car with the saggy roof hanging around my ears. But I started small, and most importantly, I *showed up* and declared myself ready. My first few goal-setting workshops had four people on average. Then 10, then 20, and now, we regularly get hundreds to a seminar. Maybe one day, thousands.

I declared myself an author way before anyone else believed I was one. I wasn't waiting for someone else to choose me, and I wasn't waiting until I felt 'anointed' by the universe. I decided that there was room for me, and yes, there's room for you too. There's room for:

❖ The introverts and extroverts

❖ The natural leaders and the more quiet followers

❖ The confident and the sensitive

❖ All ages, sizes, and backgrounds

You don't have to be the best, and you don't have to compete against anyone to be successful. Why not you, too?

— *Lesson* —

You'll never feel ready enough, and chances are that nobody is going to 'choose' you. You don't have to wait to be anointed by someone. You can choose yourself.

Be a Contributor, Not a Guru

One of the most popular posts on my blog was '37 Lessons from Becoming a Self-Made Millionaire,' and lesson number 35 was: 'I'm a contributor, not a guru.' As soon as I gave myself permission to *contribute* to the conversation about women and money, and not have to be a guru or expert on it, my business became fun. If you truly and deeply care about a topic or cause, be a contributor. Who cares if you don't know everything? You don't have to be the best to make a difference to someone.

I didn't expect the response I got to that 'lesson.' People took screenshots of it and messaged me to say how powerful it was and how relieved they were to hear that they don't have to be a guru to be successful. It resonated so deeply with people that I decided to include it in this book. And it's central to the Chillpreneur philosophy. To me, it meant that I didn't have to try so hard. Suddenly, success in business seemed attainable. I could just show up and teach what I knew, and that was enough. I didn't have to be super-special! I could be one of many voices.

When I really 'got' this, everything changed in my business. I gave myself permission to show up exactly as I am. It helped me to feel excited about offering my work to the world, to make offers to potential clients, and to extend invitations to people to join my Money Bootcamp – even though I wasn't Oprah.

I also became a lot less precious about my work because I knew it didn't have to be completely groundbreaking or unique to make a difference to the people who needed to hear it from *me.* I worried less about competitors because I cared so much about the overall mission: that women change the way they feel about money. How can I begrudge anyone talking about money, too, when we're all striving to achieve the same outcome?

I was so passionate about the topic of women and money that I didn't care about being the 'One' anymore. In fact, I realized that my voice was needed to tip the overall mission into the mainstream. The more money conversations the better, and I didn't need the ego trip of being the gatekeeper of the information.

Why *not* you, too? You're allowed to add your voice and perspective. Who's going to stop you? There's no 'cool girl' deciding who's in and who's out. Only *you* can decide if you're 'worthy' enough. And you are – but only if you choose to be.

I no longer get hugely nervous when speaking on stage, and I don't feel overwhelmed by meeting hundreds of people at events, because I know they aren't showing up to see 'me.' They want to see a representation of themselves. They want to see an example of an imperfect person choosing herself. It's attractive, compelling, and inspiring.

I'm happy to be an example and symbol for people who need to hear from me. Some like me because I'm Australian. Others like the fact that I'm not a perfect body shape. Some relate to me because I have kids. Others like my sense of humor. Whatever the reason, someone in that audience will be thinking, *If she can do it, so can I. Why not me?*

Gurus want people to follow their particular brand of 'religion,' forsaking all others. That's not what you're looking for, because it's a lot of pressure. You don't need *all the followers*, just the people who want to see and hear from *you*. Lots of people will be happy to tell you why you can't play the game. They'll say you're too young, too old, too inexperienced, too shy, too sensitive, too loud, too... *something*. But we need *all* types of leader, not just the obvious ones. Show up and fill that gap.

Why not you?

EXERCISE: WHY NOT ME?

It's helpful to listen to your own responses when you ask, 'Why not me?' Because if you're honest with yourself, you'll have a few excuses. Here are some examples.

Why not me? Because...

- I'm not experienced/credible/educated enough.
- I'm too fat/not pretty enough.

- I'm too young/old/tired.
- I have kids.
- Nobody will listen to me.
- I'm not ready.

Grab your journal and see if you can write down some more excuses.

You're not just expressing negativity for the sake of it when you identify these excuses. They will reveal valuable information that will help you uncover your business mindset issues. In fact, you can even go one layer deeper for each excuse. Take 'I'm not ready,' for example. Why am I not ready? Because:

- I need a perfect website to get started.
- I should get another qualification to prove myself first.
- I need to lose 10 pounds.

What do you do with that information? Grab your journal again and ask yourself:

- Is this true? Or is it just a story I'm making up?
- Has anyone else done this or would I be the first? (Most of the time, you can find a role model to emulate.)
- Am I putting off just getting on with it? (Most likely, yes.)
- Am I willing to choose myself anyway?

The Witch Wound, Fear, and Imposter Syndrome

*'Fearlessness is not the absence of fear. It's about
getting up one more time than we fall down.'*

ARIANNA HUFFINGTON

Joan of Arc is reported to have said, 'I am not afraid... I was born to do this.' You might not be fighting an army, but being in business is still scary! Just because you feel like it's your destiny, doesn't mean it will be smooth sailing.

A friend who was relatively new to online business sent me a text saying, 'I'm hosting a live webinar today, and I'm so scared! Tell me the fear goes away?' Um, I'm sorry, but no, it doesn't. Not entirely. But here's the good news: what scares you today won't scare you tomorrow. I can now host webinars with little stress, even though the first dozen were terrifying. Paying a six-figure tax bill isn't scary now, though I worried about paying my very first (tiny) tax bill when I started out.

At some point, with practice, everything you do in business will feel like second nature. But the first time you refuse a discount request or have to chase down a client who defaults on a payment, it's going to feel horrible, like you might actually die of fear. But you won't, and soon it will be no big deal.

And here's the bad news: there's always something new to be afraid of. Sorry! No matter how often I do it, public speaking still scares me, though it depends on the audience. Speaking to a small group is on the lower end of my fear spectrum, but people are asking me to speak to increasingly larger audiences, and that pushes me toward the middle of the spectrum. On the higher end is the idea of doing live TV interviews, which is kinda scary to me. Soon, that will be no big deal.

Why does something that seems so simple, like 'just publish a blog post' or 'just ask for the sale,' make us feel like we're literally going to *die*? I've found some good theories.

The Witch Wound

Have you ever heard of the 'Witch Wound' or the 'feminine wound?' I hadn't, until I read Lisa Lister's amazing book *Witch*; it helped me understand the fear that I and many other women experience when we start out in entrepreneurship.

According to spiritual teacher Kimberly Jones, the Witch Wound is 'the psychic scar in the collective consciousness that (mostly) women start to awaken to and feel deeply in their bodies as soon as they consider stepping into their power.'[2]

Think of your own experiences. Have you ever felt irrational terror or reluctance over something quite simple? Well, no wonder: it's never really been safe for women to speak up, display power, or create our reality without fear of persecution or conflict. Millions of women throughout history have been burned, drowned, hanged, tortured and enslaved for their beliefs, or for simply being born a girl.

Times have changed for women, but this stuff runs *deep*. Even though we're unlikely to be literally burned at the stake, it still feels dangerous to step into our power. You don't have to go very far back to see how women have been treated when they speak up. Your mother and grandmother faced a very different world than we do – one in which they had fewer rights and protections, and less respect in the workplace. And it still happens. Female politicians are called witches and bitches, and online trolls often target successful, outspoken women.

Kimberly Jones says, 'When your throat closes over when you stand up to speak or face up to authority, that's the Witch Wound closing your throat chakra. It's the shared memory of thousands of spiritual brothers and sisters being hanged and persecuted for generations of going against the grain.'[3]

Heavy, I know, but it makes sense, right? Studies are starting to reveal that we can inherit trauma from previous generations of our family,[4] and when you think about it, that makes sense, too. Passing down information about potential dangers from one generation to the next can help a species survive. It might sound far-fetched, but inherited trauma may be one of the reasons it feels so unsafe to make your voice heard by publishing a blog post or creating a simple video. Your body goes into fight-or-flight mode to keep you safe from centuries of dangerous conditions for women like us.

Life coach Natalie Ann Taggart says: 'For the longest time I couldn't figure out *why* I and the spiritual, creative women I work with felt such massive, existential fear when it came to sharing our spiritual messages. It often bordered on the point of irrational, like the time I literally felt like I was dying after I posted on Facebook or the time a client sobbed and sobbed over creating her opt-in.'[5]

Natalie says that just knowing about the collective experience of the Witch Wound can help you heal it. 'Next time you feel that resistance, that inner tug that wants to keep you safe in the status quo, recognize it as your Witch Wound. Give it love – it is protecting you. And you can choose to not be beholden to it. You can choose to heal, and to rise into the powerful magic that your soul is calling you to.'[6]

Author Seren Bertrand says, 'As women rise into their power, we face all that once held us down. We meet everything that has shamed us, blamed us, judged us. We face the long shadow of "The Inquisitor" in all the forms he or she takes. It looms large in the dark of our nightmares, our anxiety, our self-doubt.'[7]

One of my earliest memories is sitting in the welfare office with my mother, feeling terrified of the stern, besuited man and the power he had over my family and our ability to eat that month. That one experience lived with me for decades. It kept me scared about getting into trouble with authority figures like the 'taxman,' which caused me to unconsciously hold back my income for years. Starting my business made me feel incredibly vulnerable and unsafe.

And you thought you were just procrastinating! Maybe you thought you weren't qualified enough or that you needed a different background color on your website? Nope. You're breaking cycles, kicking through glass ceilings, and smashing the patriarchy! Your lizard brain thinks you're going to die, so cut yourself some slack!

> **'We are the granddaughters of the witches you weren't able to burn.'**
>
> TISH THAWER

You might not have heard of the Witch Wound until today, but I'm sure you've experienced some other fears, like:

* Fear of failure, including disappointing clients or going bankrupt

* Fear of being found out as a fraud or an imposter

* Fear of being judged or criticized

I know I have. Let me tell you again, as a self-made millionaire: *the fear never truly goes away 100 percent*. No magical revenue number makes you immune to fear. And that's okay. The absence of fear is not the goal. This is just the game of business. The goal is to use the vehicle of entrepreneurship to create more freedom, abundance, and creativity in your life and to impact the lives of others positively. That's going to come with a healthy dose of fear. It's unavoidable, but it's survivable.

Have you ever bargained with the universe about your business? 'Give me a big following, but no unsubscribes!' 'Give me Oprah-level fame, but no haters or critics!' 'Send me lots of money, but no tax bills!' Yeah, it's not going to happen. But over time, you'll gain more experience, more resources, and more resilience, which will enable you to deal with anything that gets thrown at you.

Fear of Failure

> *'A queen is not afraid to fail. Failure is*
> *another stepping stone to greatness.'*
>
> Oprah

You *will* fail in business. A lot. Some people won't like you or your work. You'll make mistakes – like sending out emails with broken links and typos. You'll f-ck up all the time, in big and little ways. When you accept that, you won't fear it, and you won't be surprised when it happens. In fact, you can plan for it.

I'm not psychic, but here are some predictions for how much you'll fail. Your sales will suck and 98 percent of people won't buy from you. (Actually, that's normal, as I'll explain later.) At least 75 percent of the customers you send newsletters to won't open them. Does that mean your emails stink? No: it has nothing to do with the quality of the content; that's just how the numbers play out. Track it over time and see – just don't think you're a failure because of it.

> *'You never lose in business. Either you win, or you learn.'*
>
> Melinda Emerson

People will complain. Whenever I create a course, I know that at least 3 percent of customers will need extra help, have complaints, or ask for a refund. It's inevitable and it has nothing to do with me. There's just no such thing as a 100 percent approval rating. That's not failure – it's statistics. Knowing that has helped me become way more chill. I know roughly how many customers will default on their payment plans and how many refund requests to expect when we do a big launch. As long as the numbers are within our predicted rates, I don't waste a minute worrying about it. You are going to have a lot of failures; it's part of doing business.

Imposter Syndrome

> *'I have written 11 books, but each time I think, "Uh-oh, they're going to find out now. I've run a game on everybody, and they're going to find me out."'*
>
> MAYA ANGELOU

Do me a favor: Google 'famous people with impostor syndrome.' You'll see that virtually everyone has it, including incredibly accomplished people.

In her book *Lean In: Women, Work, and the Will to Lead*, Sheryl Sandberg says: 'Every time I was called on in class, I was sure that I was about to embarrass myself. Every time I took a test, I was sure that it had gone badly. And every time I didn't embarrass myself – or even excelled – I believed that I had fooled everyone yet again. One day soon, the jig would be up.'[8]

In *The Secret Thoughts of Successful Women: Why Capable People Suffer from the Impostor Syndrome and How to Thrive in Spite of It*, author Valerie Young writes that Meryl Streep once told a reporter, 'You think, "Why would anyone want to see me again in a movie? And I don't know how to act anyway, so why am I doing this?"'[9] This wasn't baby Meryl speaking, either: it was after 17 Oscar nominations and 26 Golden Globe nominations!

Isn't it reassuring to know that accomplished and famous women feel the same way you do? The way I've overcome this particular fear is to forgive myself for not knowing everything, while at the same time realizing that what I *do* know can really help people. Being in business is simply sharing your gifts (knowledge and expertise) with others who don't have them. Your experiences are valuable; your opinions are useful; and someone out there needs what you have.

Women sabotage themselves by thinking they need to know everything about a topic before they teach it, or they'll be exposed as a fraud. When I started talking about money, I thought it would count only if I was as qualified to do so as financial expert Suze Orman. Otherwise, what right did I have to teach anything to do with money? And who was I to talk about living your best life if I wasn't already as successful as Oprah?

But the world needed my unique take on money. I didn't have to worry about being exposed as a fraud because I wasn't pretending to be Suze. You don't have to lead the conversation to contribute to it and honestly share your experiences. When you realize that your opinions, thoughts, and voice not only matter but are also *needed*, you can give yourself a break and just show up.

Remember, you're an expert to someone. That realization has given me so much relief. The pressure was off to be Suze (I don't look good in a blazer anyway), and there's only one Oprah. And guess what: there's only one *you*, too. Someone needs to hear *your* voice. If you show up with integrity and teach what you know with a lot of heart, you won't feel like an imposter.

Fear of Criticism

> *'To people making mean comments about my GG (Golden Globe) pics, I mos def cried about it on that private jet on my way to my dream job last night.'*
>
> ACTRESS GABOUREY SIDIBE

The fear of criticism holds so many women back. Being criticized hurts, but it's inevitable, and therefore not a valid excuse to forfeit your business dreams. *Sorry!* Do I get criticized? Yes, I'm sure I do all the time. But I don't read any unsolicited feedback about my business because honestly, I'm pretty uninterested in doing so. Why? It's none of my business what other people think of me.

Being a Chillpreneur isn't about being dismissive of negative feedback. Chillpreneurs just realize that they can't do anything to avoid it, so they shrug it off. I have friends who take criticism personally – so much so that it paralyzes them and has driven some out of business. Negative feedback isn't personal, but it's entirely unavoidable. Criticism is another statistical problem because, no matter how much you try to please everyone, you won't.

If you disagree with something I've said, that's understandable. I can often be an intolerant, bossy know-it-all. I get it. But I'm not going to expend any energy trying to change your mind. I can only be myself. And honestly, it's a colossal waste of your time to read most feedback, comments or reasons why people unsubscribed from your newsletter – because it's usually about that person's personal preference.

I can guess exactly what my negative feedback will be:

✤ You swear too much!

✤ You send too many emails.

✤ I never signed up for this! (They did.)

✤ I don't like your face/hair/voice.

Again, I'm not psychic, it's just that business is very predictable and knowing this stuff helps you not freak out when it happens. When someone says you're 'too this' or 'too that,' there's nothing you can do about it. Should you change everything about your business to accommodate everyone's preferences? No: because it's impossible! You could shorten your newsletters, and you'll still be criticized. You could change your face, and someone won't like the new one.

What's the simplest solution to overcoming the fear of being criticized? Just be yourself: it's the only thing you can do. If people like that, great; if they don't, they can find someone else. It's no big deal. You're not a perfect match for everyone. It's not your job to fix every problem in the world. That's *so exhausting.* Stand steady in who you are and attract the people who not only accept that but *love* it.

'You cannot please everyone and the effort required to
try shaves years off of your life and steals your joy.'

GAYNETÉ JONES

How to Handle Fear

So, how does a Chillpreneur deal with fear?

1. Recognize it.

2. Love and accept yourself.

You don't need to fight against it, completely change yourself, or find some way to protect yourself from it. It's going to happen. Period. Recognize that you're scared. Acknowledge that it's entirely normal. Accept that it's inevitable, predictable. As business mentor Marie Forleo says, 'everything is figureoutable.' Then, give yourself permission to be imperfect. Love and accept yourself, and move forward anyway.

EXERCISE: WHAT ARE YOU REALLY AFRAID OF?

Get out your journal and ponder the following questions until you get a juicy answer (or 10). Get specific: *what are you really afraid of?*

1. What do I worry about at 3 a.m.? (For example: getting kicked out of your community, embarrassing yourself on a global scale, attracting haters or stalkers?)

2. What's the worst thing that could happen if I moved forward in my business? (For example: are you worried about being called a fraud? About getting into trouble? Being sued? Going bankrupt? Get *specific*.)

Go deep and dirty. Get it all out. Better out than in.

Being in business is scary, but don't let fear derail you before you've even started. I hear women say, 'Oh, I'm terrified of having a big tax bill when I'm a millionaire,' and I'm like, 'Honey, just get your first client.' You'll deal with the million dollars later. You're smart and you can deal with it when it's a problem!

You might realize that some of your fears are so far in the future that you can 'park' them for a little while. It's like saying, 'Hey, Fear, you know that worry about dealing with a multimillion-dollar tax bill? Wanna come back when I'm actually a millionaire? Thanks, see you later.' And just let it go. You can't worry about everything at the same same time; focus on baby steps right now.

Rather than obsess over worries (that might not even come true), use that energy to strengthen your vision for the future. The more time you spend connecting with your dreams, the less time you'll have to think about how terrified you are! Your vision only has to be a tiny bit bigger than your fear. That's the only thing that will keep you moving forward.

Remember: fear is normal, understandable, and totally inevitable. But it's not a good excuse to stop pursuing your dreams. If you're scared, welcome to the club! Now get on with it. You don't need to be the bravest to succeed. We're all scared, but it's our time and we've got a lot of work to do.

— *Lesson* —

The Chillpreneur approach to fear is to recognize that you're scared, acknowledge that it's entirely normal, and accept that it's inevitable, predictable, and totally figureoutable. Then, give yourself permission to be imperfect.

— CHAPTER 2 —

Beliefs That Can Limit Your Success in Business

*C*hillpreneurs find the path of least resistance, which means they have to remove any obstacle that blocks their flow of abundance – otherwise known as a 'money block.' Your money blocks are the beliefs, habits, and stories that stop you from receiving money in the most natural way possible. How do you know if you have them? Everyone does: you're not the only one!

From years of working with thousands of entrepreneurs, I've acquired a pretty good sense of how these money blocks show up and how common they are. The truth is that most entrepreneurs have to work consistently at eliminating them. Including me. In business, your money blocks determine things like:

✦ **Your prices**: your ability to charge people appropriately and deal with requests for discounts.

✦ **Your money boundaries**: including how comfortable you feel chasing money that people owe you and how you deal with unreasonable refund requests.

✦ **How you spend and keep money**. This can manifest in extreme frugality or in spending every penny you make.

Dealing with your money blocks makes everything way easier, and we're Chillpreneurs, remember? The most laborious work is identifying your limiting beliefs in the first place. There are *many* types of money blocks, and you might have to do some digging to uncover yours, but I've found that those below are the most universal. You'll probably identify most strongly with one or two of them, but you might experience all three at some point.

1. You have to work really hard to make money.

2. You can help people or make money, but not both.

3. More money, more problems.

Let's look at these money blocks in turn:

Money Block #1:
You Have to Work Really Hard to Make Money

This block is probably the most common, and it's super-sneaky because hard work and busyness are culturally acceptable and in some cases, admired and encouraged. It can help you create great success for a while, but the working 'hard' part becomes self-fulfilling. There's a more natural way – the Chillpreneur way – in which you find the path of least resistance, but it will require some counterprogramming.

There's less physical work required to run a business than ever before. I don't mean to sound all old-fashioned, but it was way harder when I started my business than it is now. There were no online payment systems, making a website was either crazy-expensive or incredibly complicated, and there was hardly any automation software. It was the dark ages! (I'm kinda joking.) The fact that we now have all these relatively cheap and easy systems can bring up weird feelings because the money we can earn by using them isn't always commensurate with the amount of physical labor involved. Ease goes against an established rule in our society: an honest day's work yields an honest day's pay.

Add the internet to the mix and, suddenly, making money becomes even less onerous. You could sell an e-book to someone in China while you're sleeping. You could have someone in Sydney pay for a consultation with you (and book it on your calendar) without any back-and-forth emails. Or you could have a piece of your artwork printed onto a phone case and shipped to Ohio without being physically involved at all!

What a world we live in! And it's only going to get better. But the downside is that all this ease and flow can bring up feelings of guilt for some women. It's as if it doesn't count if we don't work really hard for it. Why? Well, we may have been told things like this from a very young age:

* 'Money doesn't grow on trees.'

* 'You don't get something for nothing.'

* 'Another day, another dollar.'

Our parents might have worked long hours for their money (unlike us) or performed hard physical labor (instead of just sitting in front of a computer). It can feel unfair to earn money without trying hard – as if we're doing something terrible or disrespecting our elders. So we sabotage ourselves by procrastinating, or we paddle upstream and make everything harder than it needs to be. We want to prove that we've earned our money through struggle and hard work, even though that's no longer necessary.

Of course, I'm not saying entrepreneurship is easy. You still have to get over your resistance, fear, and procrastination. But there's nothing you can't figure out on the internet. Most entrepreneurs aren't suffering from a lack of 'how-to': they just overcomplicate business and become too paralyzed to take action.

How Do You Know If You Have This Block?

❧ You find yourself reinventing the wheel or overcomplicating systems instead of following a proven plan.

❧ You procrastinate and end up doing things last-minute or having to pull all-nighters.

❧ You get bored and break stuff that works, just to prove you can start over from scratch.

❧ You resist delegating or outsourcing, preferring to do everything yourself because it's quicker or because nobody else can do it the way you do.

❧ You feel like you're cheating if things are too easy, or you write off your wins as flukes. You never feel proud of yourself.

Overcoming This Block

For you, there may be a shadow side to easy money. Somewhere deep inside, you may think bad things will happen if money comes with ease. I've heard women express fears such as:

❧ If I didn't work hard for it, I'd feel like I didn't earn it.

❧ I'll become lazy (and so will my kids) if things are too easy.

❧ Struggling for money is part of who I am. Who would I be without that struggle?

What comes up when you imagine money coming effortlessly? What could you do with your extra energy and resources if things *weren't* hard?

Money Block #2:
You Can Help People *or* Make Money

You might be asking the universe for more time to devote to helping more people, yet somehow feel that making money through your talents is unspiritual. Or greedy. Or weirdly inappropriate. Often, people who want to help everybody can't because they get burned out. If they allowed themselves to make money from their natural skills and talents, they could help a lot more people with ease and joy.

This is an insidious block for business success because women are conditioned to be helpful, kind, and giving without expecting anything in return, let alone money. For many women, charging people for their help feels like exploiting customers instead of selflessly giving everything away.

It's easy to undervalue our gifts, especially if what we do is fun and easy for us. As in: 'Well, it only takes me a few hours to put up a website. I shouldn't charge too much for it.' But how awesome is making money from something that's easy? It should work that way! Have you ever said, 'I don't care about the money, I just want to help people?' That sends conflicting information out into the universe.

When you believe this one at a deep level, you'll continuously prove it by attracting people who'll mirror that belief back to you. You'll get broke clients turning up asking for your help, and you'll be compelled to do so. If you don't, you'll feel like a mean bitch. You'll get haters popping up who say, 'You're just in it for the money,' and you'll feel yourself shrinking away from marketing so people won't think you're greedy.

For example, I know a lot of healers working in different modalities, such as Emotional Freedom Techniques (EFT), hypnotherapy, and Reiki, and they feel terrible about charging for their gifts. Sometimes their community reflects that back to them, saying things like, 'If you cared that much about people, this would be free,' or 'Your gift is God-given, you shouldn't charge for it.'

It's not nice to be shamed by your community. The most annoying thing is that, usually, these healers aren't charging a lot. Even when they ask for minimal contributions for things like meditations, e-books, or coaching, their audience reacts in a very unloving and outraged way. So the healer stays 'loving but broke.' Or reverts to the centuries-old practice of bartering, but instead of receiving eggs and butter, she swaps services with a friend or gets some free bookkeeping in return for her talents.

You could even use this block to feel superior to others. You might tell yourself that your business nemesis may make more money than you do (or has a book deal, or is on Oprah), but *you* really care about your *clients*, and *she* doesn't. You're selfless and she's a greedy bitch!

Or you might tell yourself that you're staying 'affordable' for people and judge the 'outrageous prices' of others. That's why this block is so sneaky. Of course, it's not mutually exclusive to care for people and charge appropriately, but on the surface, it sounds entirely reasonable and kind-hearted to keep yourself small and broke.

The most annoying thing about this money block is that the very people who should have more money (the kind, caring, and generous ones) often have the least. The paradox, of course, is that when you're broke, overstretched, or over-giving, you can't help many people. You won't have the time or energy to write your book (which could potentially help millions), or create your course (which could make you millions while transforming lives) or, at the very least, quit your soul-sucking job so you can run your business and help people full-time.

How Do You Know If You Have This Block?

✦ You feel it's exploitative to charge fees to help people transform their lives, particularly if they're struggling in some way.

✦ You feel so bad when people can't afford your fees that you work with them for free, at the expense of paying clients, or burn yourself out trying to help everyone.

✤ You feel guilty about making money, and feel like you should give it away to others.

✤ You secretly judge people in your industry who make a lot of money or think they must be doing something dodgy to be that successful.

Overcoming This Block

Attending to the needs of others is much easier when your own needs are met. The same holds true for money. Imagine how much you could benefit the world if your own needs were met and you could give from your excess?

In a *Forbes* magazine article titled 'The Rising Activism in Women's Philanthropy,' Abigail Disney – an award-winning filmmaker and philanthropist – says, 'Take the ownership of the money you have control of – stop apologizing for that; it's nothing to be ashamed of. Step into power. Ask for it. It's not going to just settle over you. This is about taking our fair share. We're half the population and we deserve half the power.'[1]

Imagine if women controlled half the money and had half the power? The world would be a very different place if we all embraced our ability to make more money.

The best way to trick this block is by connecting deeply to the transformation you could make in others if you had more money, energy, and time to devote yourself full-time to your calling. If you allowed yourself to get paid for your talents, what could you create in the world? If you weren't so tired and burned out by the un(der)paying demands of others, what would be possible in your life?

I use a pattern-interrupting mantra for this purpose: 'I serve, I deserve.' It helps me remember that giving and receiving is a virtuous circle and that it's safe for me to make money by helping others. I remind myself of all the good I do with my wealth, and that nobody is served by my staying small and broke in the world.

> *'What I learn from talking to so many women around the world: If you can empower them with the right things, the right tools, they can lift up their family. And that ultimately lifts up their community and their society.'*
>
> MELINDA GATES

Money Block #3: More Money, More Problems

People love stories about business owners or lottery winners who went broke, don't they? On the flip side, some people worry about the responsibility that would come with a windfall if they got one. For example, they fear that 'lost' family members might surface and hound them for money, or that they'll get a massive, unexpected tax bill.

The reality is that rich people have the same habits as everyone else, and often the same money problems – just on a different scale. You might judge someone who has a collection of 30 Hermès bags or a garage full of identical luxury cars, but you might have similar habits, just with crystals and dozens of identical yoga pants! (Or is that just me?)

Rich people are just like anyone else – the numbers might be different, but the behavior is the same. Rich people are just average human beings: some are nice, and some are assholes. But that doesn't mean that the richer you get, the assholier you'll get. Money just makes you richer – in money. It's not a cure-all for every problem in your life. Sure, you'll have to worry less about bills, but your fundamental personality won't change much. The truth is: if you're an asshole now, nothing will change! If you have bad habits now, money won't magically cure them. If you're a nice person, you'll just be a richer nice person.

What this block comes down to is scarcity – the worry that you can't possibly have money *and* other things you value, or that you have to give something up to be wealthier. Everyone has this belief, in slightly different ways. For example, you might think you have to give up good health, being a good parent, or having a happy marriage to be wealthier. Either way, it's not going to lead to something positive (so why would you do it to yourself?) That's why you're repelling money – because you're not 100 percent convinced it would lead to anything good.

How Do You Know If You Have This Block?

❖ You feel that having more money would come with too much responsibility, like extra taxes.

❖ You say you'd 'rather be happy than rich' (as if you can't be both).

❖ You worry that your ambition is selfish or makes you a bad mother/ partner/friend.

❖ You're afraid you'll emasculate the men in your life if you earn more money than they do.

Overcoming This Block

The problems people think money could cause are endless. I've heard things like:

❖ 'If money came easily, my family would become lazy and entitled.'

❖ 'If I had lots of money, I'd lose it somehow.'

❖ 'Everyone will judge me as a rich, greedy bitch.'

Think about the 'worst-case' scenarios you might encounter if you had more money. For example: 'Life would be too complicated.' How could more money solve that problem? It might be: 'I could hire people (such as accountants) to deal with those complications.' Or: 'Making more money would take me away from my kids, and then I'd be a bad mother.' Chillpreneurship is all about giving you *more time* with your kids, not less. But with more money, couldn't you also give your kids the experiences and tools they need to find and follow their passions?

EXERCISE: IDENTIFY YOUR MONEY BLOCKS

Grab your journal and go deep into your money blocks. What do you think you'd have to give up to be wealthier? Which of the following money blocks resonates with you the most?

- You have to work really hard to make money.
- You can help people *or* make money, but not both.
- More money, more problems.

If you want to go even deeper into the conversation around money blocks, I suggest you read my last book, *Get Rich, Lucky Bitch* after you finish this one, and consider joining my Money Bootcamp.

— CHAPTER 3 —

Millionaire Mindset Lessons

ecoming a millionaire doesn't really make you special or clever, but the truth is that my biggest secret for becoming one is to focus on some very specific mindset upgrades; these can be summed up as follows:

1. There's always more money.

2. There are easier ways to make money.

3. Know thyself and prosper.

4. A wealthy woman looks like you.

Mindset Lesson #1: There's Always More Money

> *'If you approach the ocean with a cup, you can only take away a cupful; if you approach it with a bucket, you can take away a bucketful.'*
>
> RAMANA MAHARSHI

One of the cornerstones of the Chillpreneur philosophy is that there's always more. There's enough for everyone, and we live in a world of abundance. This is the first mindset lesson I want you to master: *There's always more money.*

Of course, it doesn't always feel like that. I'm not saying income inequality isn't real, and that there's no poverty in the world. But chances are that *you* have every opportunity to change your circumstances. Wealthy women are great for the planet, yet we still hold ourselves back. One way we keep ourselves small is by thinking that the world is a zero-sum game: if I win, someone else is going to lose; if I'm successful, it will be at someone else's expense.

But that's not true. You can do some amazing things with your wealth; there's no limit to what you can dream; and there's no cap on your earning potential if you're willing to do the work necessary in your business.

Never had this been so apparent to me, and in such a hilariously literal way, than when I was freaking out about buying our dream house. It had taken years to manifest and finally the day came. Instead of feeling great, I was experiencing what psychologist and author Gay Hendricks calls an 'upper limit problem,' which is the feeling that we've hit our capacity for success. It can feel like resistance, guilt, or even the sense that we're about to get into trouble.

It was as if I'd only just realized what a massive manifestation we'd pulled off. Just six weeks earlier, we didn't have all the money we needed to buy the house, and part of me still didn't believe we'd done it, even though we'd just completed the most successful launch we'd ever had. I felt sick: had we bitten off more than we could chew? Who did I think I was? Could we really afford this house in this swanky neighborhood?

All these thoughts swirling around in my head cast a dark cloud over what should have been a day of celebration. (This is normal, by the way. I call it a 'success hangover,' which is when something that's supposed to feel good has the opposite effect, and you feel weirdly guilty or bad.)

During the car ride to our new property, I said to my husband Mark, 'Babe, we're going to have to be so careful about money this year. With the new house to build, another baby and two mortgages, we'll really have to tighten our belts.'

Mark looked at me in surprise and said, 'That doesn't sound like you!' I'm usually the more optimistic of the two of us when it comes to reaching big goals, and because I teach money mindset, he'd never heard me talk so negatively before. But I was spooked about this big dream coming true, and it didn't feel good.

I let out the breath I was holding and said, 'You're right: there's always more money.' At that very moment, a shower of money hit the windshield of our car: at least $1,000 in $50 notes flew at us like confetti. Yes, really. This story isn't metaphorical. Actual money hit our car! The windshield wipers came on, and the notes bounced and scattered all over the road, blowing into the trees lining the highway. We both screamed involuntarily and said simultaneously, 'Did you see that?'

Then I said, 'Did that really happen?' We were both hysterical. 'Should we pull over?' Mark asked. I still couldn't quite believe what had happened, especially at the very moment I'd affirmed out loud that 'There's always more money.' But I knew that it was a big message from the universe.

'The actual money isn't the point,' I replied, 'and I definitely don't want to scrabble around on this busy highway to collect money that doesn't belong to us. The lesson is that there's always more money, and we're going to be fine.' We both started laughing because it was just too weird.

Was it a shared hallucination? All I know is that it was divine timing. Just at that moment of doubt and scarcity, the universe decided to remind me that there's *always* more money. There's always enough. And just like that, I felt incredible about the new property purchase. I decided to live in a world of abundance, not scarcity. To this day, I've no idea how it happened. Maybe someone was about to buy something in cash, and it accidentally blew out the window. Who knows? I've never heard another person from my town mention it. I still laugh about the divine timing, and I hope you remember it too.

There's always enough.

There Are Always Enough Clients

How many clients do you need to replace your day job or have a successful, thriving business? Seriously. Run the numbers and figure it out. And if you increase your prices or streamline your business, you might need even fewer. With so many billions of people in the world, there are a lot of potential customers looking for exactly what you can deliver. And you need only a tiny percentage of them to buy! There are always enough clients.

There Are Always More Opportunities

So, you missed out on an important project or speaking gig. Who cares? There are a million other conferences to go to, and more clients that will probably suit you better, so breathe and let go of your fear of missing out. There are always more opportunities.

There Are Always More Ideas

So, your practice business didn't pan out. That doesn't mean you're a failed entrepreneur: it simply means you're an entrepreneur! Think how many Virgin offshoots Sir Richard Branson has tried out (Virgin Brides or Virgin Cola, anyone?). If Branson understands anything, it's that ideas are abundant and, if one doesn't work, there's always another one around the corner.

There's Always More Time

So many women feel an internal urgency to do *all the things* right now. For example, how many potential book ideas are rattling around in your head (at least three for me) and feeling like they all need to be birthed *right now*? You can be in only one stage of pregnancy at a time. Let it all unfold in perfect, divine timing.

Paradoxically, I've found that, when I take the attitude of 'abundant time,' I get a lot more done! If I take the pressure off myself to do everything, I naturally find myself being more productive. Maybe when you're not forcing yourself, you won't get as bogged down in resistance and procrastination.

— *Lesson* —

There's always enough money, and acquiring more of it won't deprive others of wealth.

Mindset Lesson #2:
There Are *Easier Ways* to Make Money

'I intentionally abandoned the hard stuff early on because not only do I think it's useless, I think it's a distraction.'

SETH GODIN

When I was a teenager, there was a nationwide competition to win a new car. The catch was that you had to live in it with four other people. Whoever stayed in the car the longest, got to keep it. You were given a bathroom break every two hours and could order any fast food you wanted, but all the rubbish had to stay in the car, and you had to sleep there too. No showers, either. You stayed in it until you couldn't handle it any longer.

The car visited my local shopping mall as part of the promotion. It was before reality shows became a big thing on TV, so I was excited to check it out. By then, the contest had been going on for two weeks, and they were down to a few determined (and very smelly) contestants. Onlookers took turns to gawk in the window at these poor people, who were sitting in their own filth, wanting to win the car.

I think about that competition often because, first of all, who wants a car after it's been lived in like that, and second, there are easier ways to get a new car. Just buy one! Because I teach manifestation, often people ask me how they can win a competition to go on vacation or win a house through a raffle, and I think, *Just work on your business and buy what you want.* That counts too! You don't always have to win things.

Entrepreneur and author Seth Godin famously said, 'When in doubt, raise money from your customers by selling them something they truly need – your product.' Go get more clients and buy what you want.

That car story relates to the second of my mindset lessons: 'There are *easier ways* to make money.' I say this all the time when I find myself doing the opposite: overcomplicating things, pursuing an idea that's not exactly in my zone of genius, or otherwise making things harder for myself. Maybe you do the same.

In the pursuit of the entrepreneurial dream, we often take the hardest route. A lot of my early businesses failed – not because the ideas weren't good, but because they felt hard for me, and I just wanted the outcome (the money). I didn't care about the business at all. And sometimes, I pursued a good idea that wasn't really a natural fit for me.

Are You Solving the Right Problem?

Years ago, when I was still desperately looking for my 'thing' (otherwise known as a calling or purpose), I read a book that said, 'Solve a problem that you're passionate about.' I was passionate about a lot of things, but want to know what was really pissing me off at the time? The lack of hooks in public bathroom stalls.

Every time I went into a public restroom, I'd get frazzled about where to put my giant coat, hat, scarf, and gloves (I was living in London at the time and wore lots of layers), not to mention the enormous handbag I carried around. I'd recently read a study that revealed how dirty people's handbags are. *Wow*, I thought, *this is my cause!* It seemed perfect for my pedantic and fastidious Virgo ways. Plus, complaining seemed to channel my energy into changing things for the better.

So, to market my new 'toilet hook' business, I thought I'd start with a name-and-shame letter campaign to businesses, and then progress to an app featuring a map of all the 'Denise-approved' restrooms where hooks were provided. Women would thank me in droves. Fewer employees would call in sick; productivity would improve. It was life-changing stuff! I was *outraged* about this issue. I had no idea how to monetize it (that didn't seem to matter), but it was obviously something that was needed in the world, and I was the girl to do it.

So, I enthusiastically told a friend about the idea. He listened to my entire rant, and when I finished, he calmly said, 'Why don't you carry around a bag of stick-on hooks, and when you're in a bathroom without one, just stick one on.' Mind blown. It was just so... zen.

In an instant, this guy had wiped my 'brilliant business idea' off the map. I looked at him, dumbfounded. 'But what am I supposed to do with my life?' I asked. I seriously thought that my entrepreneurial dreams were dead.

'Denise, you're a storyteller,' he said. 'Tell stories.' So that's what I do. I write a blog. I speak on stages. I author books. I basically make a living by telling random stories and inspiring women to create the life they want. It's so much easier than being the 'Toilet Hook Queen.'

I'm so grateful to my friend because, instead of rolling his eyes at my dumb business idea, he could see that underneath my 'toilet problem' was a real desire to change the world. It was a massive weight off my shoulders to hear that I didn't have to solve everything, and that my real gift was inspiring others to find their passion.

I'd thought that aligning myself with a simple, annoying problem would be great. But it was the wrong problem. It's so tempting to try and solve all the problems you encounter and to turn every emerging passion into a business! At networking events, people sometimes tell me about their latest business idea, and I just want to interrupt and say, 'Honey, that sounds way too hard. There are easier ways to make money!'

Maybe you're overcomplicating things; maybe you're going into the wrong industry, trying to help the wrong people, or pursuing a business that's simply the wrong fit for your skills and talents. There is a path of least resistance: you just have to find it. Remember:

❖ You don't have to pursue random business ideas.

❖ You don't have to buy all the catchy domain names.

❖ It's okay to just let hobbies be hobbies (in fact, turning a hobby into a business can take the joy right out of it).

❖ You can be an activist for change without turning your activism into a business.

If you don't solve a problem, don't worry, someone else will – you can count on it. Other people created products like Loo Hooks, Hero Clips, and Bagnets to deal with the toilet hook problem. Thanks to them, I'm not trapped talking about toilet hooks for the rest of my life.

You'll have to learn this lesson over and over: there are easier ways to make money! Deciding not to pursue an idea doesn't mean it isn't important to you. You can:

❖ Care about something deeply, sign a petition, write a letter or make a donation, but not make it your business.

❖ Contribute to someone else's crowd-funding campaign without making it your business.

❖ Have a really fantastic business idea without making it *your* business.

Saying 'no' to a good idea (like toilet hooks) is a hard lesson to learn, but if you don't, you can't focus on your real purpose. There are easier ways to make money than to:

* Follow a path that's not yours.

* Work with people you can't really help, even though you think you should.

* Solve a problem that someone else can solve.

Mindset Lesson #3: Know Thyself and Prosper

*'If you don't know yourself, you can't
live the life of your dreams.'*

IYANLA VANZANT

People are always surprised when I tell them I'm an introvert. They say things like, 'But you film so many videos!' 'But you're so bubbly and confident!' 'But you have a big business!'

Yes, but I make those videos alone in my home. No human interaction needed. Yes, I can be bubbly on stage, because I've learned how to protect my energy between speaking gigs (and take days to recover from them.) Yes, I have a big business, because it's set up to enhance my strengths. I've outsourced and delegated my weaknesses and embraced the Chillpreneur philosophy of 'there are easier ways to make money.'

The internet is a perfect business vehicle for introverts. You can run a global business without having to interact directly with other people. In fact, you can work in your pajamas every day if you want to (and I do, a lot). But this chapter isn't about being an introvert (that's a whole other book). It's about uncovering *your* unique superpowers and using them to create your ideal life and business. That's the third mindset lesson to master. There's a path of least resistance for you, and your job is to find it. How? *Know thyself*:

+ Understand how and why you sabotage yourself.

+ Discover what kind of work is fun and easy for you.

+ Know your warning signs of burnout.

The Chillpreneur way is to know yourself so profoundly that work doesn't feel like work – it feels like a natural extension of your personal preferences. The Chillpreneur way is to find the logical path (for you) and reduce any unnecessary friction in your life and business. That doesn't mean it's smooth sailing every minute of the day. I still get scared to go outside my comfort zone, but I'm mindful of doing things that work with my personality and not against it.

In their book *The Astonishing Power of Emotions*, Esther and Jerry Hicks expand this into an upstream/downstream analogy: '… feel for a moment the sensation of relief that you would experience if you had been paddling against the current in an upstream direction and then suddenly just stopped paddling, in an attitude of giving in to the stream and letting it just turn you and take you downstream.'[1]

Going with the flow doesn't mean you'll never work. I work a lot, and when I'm not working, I'm often *thinking* about my work. But it doesn't feel stressful to me (most of the time). Occasionally, I get out of balance, but it doesn't take long to switch direction, make some tweaks and float downstream again. The first step is to *know who you are*. The second step is to *accept it lovingly*, knowing that your personality is perfect for you and your business.

> *'Making the decision to not follow a system, or someone else's rules, has allowed me to really dig into what my own strengths and gifts are without spending time feeling jaded or wasteful.'*
>
> Ishita Gupta

We're all different for a reason. Thank God there are people who have figured out how bridges stay up and planes fly because that isn't my bag. But the world would be a little boring if it was full of only engineers. It needs creative people, too. It needs dreamers and organizers and listeners and artists and visionaries of all types.

There's a spot in the world that's exactly your size and shape, so there's no point wishing you were different. The idea behind personal development isn't to change everything about yourself; it's about polishing your true, inherent beauty. Self-acceptance is way more profitable than self-help. Knowing more about your real personality – mainly how it expresses around money and business – will help you to:

✦ Make or save more money naturally, without feeling like you have to work harder than necessary or sell out.

✦ Attract clients who naturally want what you're giving. You'll stop twisting yourself into knots trying to please everyone, which is a surefire recipe for failure and dissatisfaction.

✦ Experience less friction in your life and business. You'll feel like you're in the flow and won't have to 'force' yourself to do anything.

✦ Trust your own decisions and not follow the herd or be tempted to try the latest marketing fad.

You're Enough: Exactly As You Are

I honestly spend zero time these days working on my weaknesses. It's so much easier to maximize my strengths and not try to change my fundamental personality. That's way too hard, and a waste of energy. I know this goes against the grain of personal development, but I see too many entrepreneurs wasting time on overcoming their weaknesses for marginal returns. They take course after course or pursue yet another certification (procrasti-learning!)

You're way better off outsourcing, delegating, or eliminating the impact of weaknesses altogether than you are changing your behavior (more on this later). Remember: pursue the path of least resistance. Yes, you can adapt, but you really can't escape your natural personality type. Chill out and accept it.

> *'Wherever you go, there you are.'*
> CONFUCIUS

That doesn't mean you can't change habits or beliefs. That's something entirely different. I've been able to change my mindset to be more optimistic and positive, but I always fall back into certain personality traits, and that's been true no matter which job or industry I've tried.

This theme will come up again and again. Later, I'm going to encourage you to find the business model that feels easy to you, the clients that are the most pleasurable to deal with, and the marketing techniques that feel the most natural, regardless of what other people are doing.

That's the Chillpreneur way. It's not about being lazy – it's just going with the flow for maximum results. And guess what? You might resist it – because it feels too easy or obvious, or because your business guru told you it had to be a certain way. But their way might not be the best for *you*, and you need to do some self-exploration to figure out what works better. The path to Chillpreneurship begins by giving yourself permission to be exactly the way you are.

> *'You can't stop the waves, but you can learn to surf.'*
> JON KABAT-ZINN

You could use your newfound self-awareness to make micro-shifts in your business: for example, in the types of client you work with, the products and services you offer, the branding you use, the team you hire, and the processes you run your whole business around. Don't throw the baby out with the bathwater, though. Just make little tweaks to create more pleasure and less friction.

What Feels Good?

A really simple question to ask yourself is, 'What feels good?'

* 'What kind of clients do I enjoy working with most?'

* 'What work feels best to me?'

* 'What did I like about my last project?'

When things feel bad, you have to learn from it, too. For example, as a favor to a friend, I gave a keynote speech at her conference – to an entirely different audience than usual, one that wasn't even close to my target market. Although the speech was well received, I came off stage feeling *horrible* and used up. As if I'd pimped myself out for someone else's gratification.

Each time something feels good or bad, you can adjust your business in big and small ways. You can re-evaluate your target audience (and change up your marketing accordingly). You can put boundaries in place (for example, I now have a speaking request form that spells out the type of audience I'm right for), or you can eliminate product or service offerings. You have permission to make things easier or more pleasurable for yourself!

— *Lesson* —

The secret to success is to know yourself: know what makes you tick, how you sabotage yourself, and what your path of least resistance is.

How to Know Yourself Better

It can take years, if not decades, to know yourself better by making mistakes and harvesting the lessons they offer. I've found that the quickest and easiest way is by taking personality tests, such as Myers-Briggs, Kolbe, the Enneagram, StrengthsFinder, etc., and applying the lessons directly to my business.

For example, I found out that I'm a 'High Quick Start' in the Kolbe test, which means I take action very quickly, love spontaneity, and don't need a lot of preparation to get started. I just thought I was impatient and lazy! I actually work best off the cuff. Once I realized that this was actually one of my strengths, I embraced it. I know my stuff, and I can run a three-day conference with virtually no agenda or notes. I've stopped beating myself up over it, and that's such a relief!

I think you can learn something from almost any personality test, even if it's not designed specifically for business. The goal is self-knowledge for more pleasure and profit, and less stress or friction. For example, I loved the book *The Five Love Languages* by Gary Chapman. It's about love relationships, but I could also apply it to my business.

Chapman says there are five ways that you express and prefer to receive love.[2] They are: receiving gifts, quality time, words of affirmation, acts of service, and physical touch. My love language is quality time (such as sitting on the couch watching a movie with Mark, but *not talking* to each other) and acts of service (I love that Mark cooks most of our meals). Knowing that about myself means I need to make sure I don't have to work evenings or weekends. Otherwise, I'll feel resentful toward my clients and business for cutting into my couch-not-talking-time with Mark!

You can learn just as much from your preferred way of being as you can from your least favorite way. For example, words of affirmation are not important to me. I just don't need to hear praise – in fact, it often makes me feel uncomfortable. In applying this to my business, I asked my team not to forward gushing emails from clients. It just feels like a distraction. I want to stay in my Chillpreneur flow, regardless of what others think of me. However, this isn't a good thing in that I often resist asking for and displaying testimonials in my business. Thankfully, my team collects them instead – we've built it into the business system.

Gifts also hold little value for me, so I ask people not to send me thank-you presents. Again, some personalities would *love* receiving presents. I don't, and I've put boundaries in place because of it.

You can use any personality test to create more ease and flow in your business, but sometimes you have to dig a little deeper to see how it relates to money. The best personality test I've found for uncovering money beliefs is the Sacred Money Archetypes® assessment. I loved it so much that I became certified in teaching the method, and it's been life-changing for my clients and Money Bootcamp participants.

The results tell you precisely how your blend of personality can make and keep more money, so you find your exact path to more wealth. I'm a Ruler, Maverick, and Romantic. My sabotages are a tendency to overwork, take risks, and ignore details about money! You might be an Alchemist, Accumulator, Celebrity, Connector, Romantic, or Nurturer. This is seriously one of the best insights into your money personality and can help you figure out your strengths and weaknesses when it comes to finances.

You can learn what your archetypes are and get a free Sacred Money Archetypes® personality report at Chillpreneur.com/Bonus. Do the quiz now; it takes around 15 minutes and will give you some incredible insights into your personality and how you can create more effortless profit.

EXERCISE: IDENTIFY YOUR STRENGTHS AND WEAKNESSES

In your journal, write down the first answer to the following questions that comes to mind. Don't think about it too much. As you go through the book, you'll get a lot more clarity about how you'll want to design your life and business going forward.

WHAT ARE YOUR TOP STRENGTHS?

1. List your top three.

2. Describe *one* thing in your business that you can change this week to take advantage of those three strengths.

3. Make that change (aim for a micro-change, rather than something dramatic).

WHAT ARE YOUR TOP WEAKNESSES?

1. List your top three.

2. Describe *one* thing in your business that you can change this week to minimize your weaknesses.

3. Make that change (again, pick something small to act on).

Mindset Lesson #4:
A Wealthy Woman Looks Like You

> *'Women get mixed messages in childhood: You can
> do anything you want... but it wouldn't hurt to
> find someone who will take good care of you.'*
>
> LOIS P. FRANKEL

One of the most powerful speakers I've ever heard was Suze Orman at the Hay House 'I Can Do It!' conference. Suze introduced her speech by saying, slowly and deliberately: 'I stand before you a very, very, *very* wealthy woman.' It gave me goose bumps.

Her words stuck with me because I'd never heard a woman claim her wealth and success like that before. Bragging isn't generally seen as a positive trait in women, but what was so compelling about

Suze's declaration was that it was so matter-of-fact and made without apology.

The final mindset lesson is giving yourself permission to be wealthy and successful, exactly as you are now. Most of us have a perception of what 'wealthy' means, and it's probably really outdated. Part of working through your money blocks is identifying your money stories and limiting beliefs. In this section, we're going one layer deeper, into claiming ourselves as wealthy women.

When you Google 'define wealth,' some of the definitions[3] include: an abundance of valuable possessions or money; a plentiful supply of a particular desirable thing; wellbeing. Well, what if you're a minimalist and don't want an abundance of possessions – can you still be wealthy? What if you care deeply about the environment – doesn't being wealthy come with a big carbon footprint? What if you hate fancy clothes and have no desire to buy a big house or an expensive car – does that mean you won't have a big enough 'why' to generate more money?

Not at all, but it's going to take some deprogramming because, in our society, we often get incredibly mixed messages about wealth. Money becomes a personal attribute or failing, and wealthy people are often perceived as more clever, ambitious, and hardworking than the average person. You might have very fixed (but misguided) views about what a wealthy woman looks like.

I talk openly about being wealthy because I want to showcase a young(ish) self-made millionaire who is a reasonably nice person (most of the time), and dresses, looks, and acts like an average person. I'm just not that fancy, and honestly, I think it disappoints some people that I'm not living a more glamorous life. I drive a mid-range minivan full of sand and McDonald's crumbs; I'm not impressed by super-fancy restaurants; I own very few expensive shoes, handbags, or clothes; and I'm just boringly normal.

Nobody who meets me would automatically think I'm rich, and most of the advisors Mark and I meet automatically assume he's the breadwinner in our family (I put them straight pretty quickly). Most people have a fixed idea in their mind about what 'rich' looks like. I know I still do (an older white lady at the country club wearing white or beige linen clothes, gold leather sandals, lots of gold jewelry and with blonde, perfectly coiffed hair).

In reality, there's no dress requirement for wealth! Steve Jobs wore jeans and a black turtleneck practically every day, and Mark Zuckerberg wears jeans and a grey T-shirt. My style? Chillpreneur. My summer uniform is shorts and a caftan, and my winter uniform is jeans and a caftan. But you can do it your way! You can pick and choose the kind of wealthy woman you want to be. You can mix high-end and low-end. Who cares? There aren't any rules about how to be rich anymore, and together, we're changing the conversation so other women can join us.

If you want to open your eyes to 'real wealth' rather than 'TV wealth,' read *The Millionaire Next Door: The Surprising Secrets of America's Wealthy* by Thomas J. Stanley and William D. Danko. It offers an extensive study of wealthy people and identifies seven common traits. They're not what you think! 'Many people who live in expensive homes and drive luxury cars do not actually have much wealth,' the authors say. 'Many people who have a great deal of wealth do not even live in upscale neighborhoods.'[4]

This book changed my view about who I had to be in order to make more money because the more-is-better lifestyle just didn't sit well with me. I thought I had to 'fake it until I made it,' but I discovered that designer stuff just wasn't my bag (literally). I'm not judging people who love fancy things (a lot of my friends do) – I just realized that it wasn't for me, and that's okay. I could redefine wealth *my way* and so can you.

By the way, Stanley wrote two follow-ups that are just as good: *Millionaire Women Next Door*, and *Stop Acting Rich ... And Start Living Like A Real Millionaire* – both highly recommended for helping redefine what wealth means to you.

'Money should never change one's values....
Making money is only a report card. It's
a way to tell how you're doing.'

Thomas J. Stanley

If you ignore all the other money blocks and try to get to the core of the issue, you'll find many women think that being wealthy just isn't their destiny – that they somehow lack a magical ingredient. What do *you* think that magical ingredient is? Intelligence? Ambition? Hard work? Great grooming?

It could be all of those things, but I've met some dumb people who are wealthy. I've met humble wealthy women who don't consider themselves overly ambitious or competitive, and I've also met a lot of Chillpreneurs who don't work that hard, love what they do, and have a healthy work/life balance.

Maybe you think you have to look or act a certain way? Get honest and dig deep to find out what you think you have to change about yourself to be a wealthy woman – your hair/face/skin/clothes/house/car/weight?

Exercise: What Does a Rich Woman Look Like?

Visualizing the rich

Close your eyes for a minute and conjure up what you think a 'rich woman' looks like. What is she wearing? (Do you actually know anyone who dresses like that, or is it a cliché from TV?) What are her defining characteristics? How old is she?

Write it all down in your journal, and then do the same exercise for how you perceive a 'successful entrepreneur' looks. Is it the same? Or different?

VISUALIZING YOURSELF AS RICH

Stand in front of a mirror and say to yourself, 'This is what a wealthy woman looks like.' In your journal, write down what comes up for you. Does it feel weird? Braggy, arrogant, untrue, impossible?

Don't be afraid of the little voice that answers, because it's just giving you an insight into your beliefs. Ask it, 'Why *else* can't I be rich?'

The more you do this exercise, and the more you decide to claim for yourself the mantle of a wealthy woman, the more you'll start to believe that it's possible for someone like you. Because, guess what? There are no height, weight, or skin color requirements for wealth. You don't have to look or sound a certain way. There's no dress code, purity test, or other conformity required. There's only what we tell ourselves.

Now, I'm not saying that you won't face some challenges, or that it's easy for everyone. There are real discriminatory problems in the world that make it harder for some women than others, but it's not *impossible*. It's probably already been done, so why not you, too? You are what a wealthy woman *can* look like, especially now. There's nothing about you that precludes you from being rich. You can be wealthy and wear sweats every day, if you want. You can be rich and kind. You can be rich and normal. You can be as rich and as fabulous as you want.

Go and look for wealthy role models who have a similar life story to your own, or who look like you. They'll help you believe it's possible. And if you can't find any, guess what? It's *your* job to fill that gap! It's your destiny to be a money role model for other women. Has nobody done it from your town, country, industry, or with your accent? Then it's *your* job!

You can feel scared by that, but as author and activist Glennon Doyle says, 'We can do hard things.' And honestly, the journey is not going to be anywhere near as scary as you think. You're not alone. You're part of an ever-growing community that's completely redefining what it means to be a wealthy woman because we know the world needs us. You *are* what a wealthy woman looks like.

No Man's Land

'We are the ones we've been waiting for.'

JUNE JORDAN

Did you watch Patty Jenkin's movie *Wonder Woman*? It kinda blew my mind, especially the scenes where Diana (Wonder Woman) goes off to fight 'The War.' Her love interest, Steve Trevor, says to her: 'This war is a great big mess, and there's not a whole lot you and I can do about that. I mean, we can get back to London and try to get to the men who can.' Diana shakes her head at this and says: *'I am the man who can.'*

Then, as all the soldiers are waiting in the trenches, Diana urges them to rise up and fight. Steve says, 'This is no man's land, Diana! It means no man can cross it.' Of course, she ignores him and climbs the ladder out of the trench, ready and determined to go into battle to save the world.

The words 'no man's land' hit me as a massive call to action. I felt all my excuses about my business fall away. The people who created the problems of the world won't fix them, and there's a new generation of leaders who have to step into that void. We can reject the 'old rules' of engagement. If we want a better world, we have to make it happen ourselves. My business can be part of the solution and so can yours. **I am the (wo)man who can.**

What's Your No Man's Land?

> *'Success doesn't come to you, you go to it.'*
> MARVA COLLINS

How can you work up the courage to fit in where there are no voices, faces, or perspectives like yours? What combination of skills and talents do you have that allows you into previously forbidden spaces?

We think some rules bar us from entry, but the rules have changed so much that no one really knows what they are anymore. Nobody can tell you 'no,' but waiting for permission means you'll wait forever. Maybe your no man's land is just having the audacity to show up exactly as you are.

— *Lesson* —

We are the ones who can. We are the
ones we have been waiting for.

💡 The Big Idea

If you remember nothing else from Part I, remember this: *Mindset is the only thing that matters. Believe that there's always enough, there's always more, and most importantly, that you are enough.* You are what a wealthy woman looks like. If not you, then who?

— PART II —

Business
Models

— CHAPTER 4 —

The Keyless Life

'It is always the simple that produces the marvelous.'
AMELIA BARR

The truth is that we make business way more complicated than it needs to be. Myself included. Yep, I don't always have it together: I often create unnecessary work for myself, resist making things easy, reinvent the wheel, and frequently change my mind midway through a project (driving my team, including Mark, crazy).

I'm not perfect, but I've created a pretty chilled million-dollar business without burning myself out (too much) and without massive staff or overheads, and I want to share all the details with you, including how I set up my home life to support my business and vice versa. Most business books ignore the home stuff because, frankly, they are written by men who don't have to think about it too much. The reality for a lot of women is that our business and home lives are intertwined and impact each other, especially if we work from home or have a family. I call this philosophy 'the keyless life.'

When I first had kids, the simplest things suddenly felt *really hard*. Like getting in and out of the car with a diaper bag, handbag, shopping bags, and an actual baby (or two). With kids *and* a business, life suddenly seemed complicated and overwhelming, and I felt I'd lost my easy-breezy, chilled personality. Instead, I became a frazzled 'busy mom'!

When I bought a new car, I was excited to see it had keyless entry, which meant that, as long as the car key was somewhere on my person (usually covered in crumbs at the bottom of my bag), I could get into the car without needing a spare hand to fish it out. It was just one tiny thing off my mind, but it made a huge difference to my life.

Then I decided to change all my card PINs to the same number. It's never been an issue or security concern, and has saved me hours of angst, especially when I've got pregnancy or baby brain. I then bought phone chargers for every room in the house, and multiple headsets, so we stopped arguing about who was 'stealing' them from whom. I turned off my voicemail because I hated listening to messages. I got a meal delivery service, so I actually ate lunch every day. I got a water filter for my office. I deliberately looked for ways to make my daily life easier. Most of these upgrades were either free or very inexpensive but they made a huge difference.

Then I had another idea! I replaced our front door locks with electronic keypads, which meant I never had to find my keys again and could enter the house easily with a code. Again, a tiny thing that changed my daily experience. Between the keyless entry on the house and car, I haven't had to use a set of keys in years! Thus, a *keyless life*.

Now I extend that same philosophy to the rest of my life and business. I ask, 'How could I make this as easy and stress-free as possible?' and 'What little, annoying things can I eliminate from my daily life?' Creating a 'keyless life' is so much fun, and I'm constantly looking for new ways to create simplicity and ease. So please, if you're inspired by this chapter, tag me on social media @denisedt using the hashtag #keylesslife and let me know how you're implementing it in your own life.

This philosophy doesn't have to be literal. You don't have to throw away your keys or change the PIN for your ATM card (some people will hyperventilate at those suggestions). The idea is to reduce any unnecessary friction in your daily life, so you can use your energy for other things, including making more money or taking a break every now and then. You can apply simplification to any business so you can create more joy, energy, and profit without working so hard. That's what being a Chillpreneur is all about, and if you need permission, I'm here to help!

> *'Be a curator of your life. Slowly cut things out*
> *until you're left only with what you love, with*
> *what's necessary, with what makes you happy.'*
> LEO BABAUTA

What Is a 'Business Model'?

In this chapter, we'll see how you can find the path of least resistance in all areas of your business model. It's not about being lazy; it's just maximizing your energy for the things that are important to you. So, what is a business model? It just means how you do things in your business. For example:

* What kind of products or services you offer, and how you actually deliver them.

* Your target market and your marketing.

* How you run your business (for example, your systems and team).

You can apply the keyless life philosophy to all these areas, and that's when life becomes way more relaxed. Of course, you'll still have your normal ups and downs (this is a practice after all, and we're not aiming for perfection), but the idea is to craft your business and life in a way that's perfectly tailored for you – for where you are right now and where you want to go.

So many women start their business journey believing there's only one right way to do business. You might think that if you just figure out what that model is, you'll somehow have it made. You've probably even invested in various courses or coaching with business gurus to try and figure out the silver-bullet formula. Or maybe you think you have to copy someone else's business model because it looks so effortless from the outside. I get this a lot. Because I'm pretty chill about business, and my business is financially successful, people often try to emulate my way of doing things.

But it doesn't work like that. Why? The 'best' business model is just the one that works best for *you*. And that takes self-awareness, self-discovery, and a willingness to experiment and find *your* version of a Chillpreneur business. What's easy for me might be hard for you, and vice versa. What feels good and gives me energy might give you stress hives! This is basically why I don't give specific business advice anymore. My answer is always 'it depends,' and then I ask people questions about their personality or their Sacred Money Archetype®. It's totally okay to create a business that feels good for you, even if you resist the ease at first.

The Keyless Life Business

How do you know if your business is in alignment with your keyless life?

+ **It's the right fit, personality-wise**. Each aspect of your business suits your innate talents, preferences, and skill set. You're in flow most of the time (even if some things are out of your comfort zone). Everything else is eliminated, automated, or delegated (more on this coming up).

+ **'Enoughness.'** You find the sweet spot between contentment and ambition. You still have big goals, but you have pride and gratitude for what you've created, so you don't have a constant nagging feeling of not having done enough. You don't beat yourself up for mistakes, and see them as important rites of passage.

✤ **The courage to pivot**. When things aren't working for you anymore, you recognize that your business plays by your rules and serves your life, not the other way around. Not every business lasts a lifetime. You understand the season of the business lifecycle you're in.

✤ **Simplicity**. Even if your business is complex, you don't try to solve everyone's problems; you're clear on what you do, who you can help, and how you make money. You don't reinvent the wheel or overcomplicate things for the sake of it.

✤ **Sustainability.** You don't work yourself or your team into the ground. You have a long-term view of your business and know that you'll go through seasons of growth as well as plateaus. You try and plan these in to respect the seasons of your life, rather than being buffeted by change or circumstance.

✤ **An attitude of abundance.** You make a healthy profit by charging what you're worth and creating win-win partnerships for yourself, your clients, suppliers, and community. Basically, you make more than enough money to support yourself, your family, and the causes that are important to you, without guilt or shame.

The Keyless Personal Life

And how does it work in your personal life?

✤ **Giving yourself permission not to be perfect in every area** – the perfect wife, mother, community member, or volunteer. You accept all aspects of who you actually are, not just who you think you should be.

✤ **Rewriting the rules of what you 'should' do** – as a woman, wife, mother, daughter, role model, and friend. This includes guilt-free outsourcing at home, setting boundaries around your time and energy, and allowing yourself to carve your own path, regardless of what other people think.

+ **Giving yourself space for pleasure in your life** – including time for creativity, rest, relaxation, and expression of the things that fulfill you. It means making your health, wellbeing, and personal fulfillment a priority and protecting yourself.

+ **Accepting your true desires** – regardless of what other people want. You live where and how you want to live, and accept all your goals as valid. You don't judge yourself for being too ambitious or not ambitious enough. You practice self-love, compassion, and acceptance.

This list is obviously aspirational (for me too): so don't lose heart by trying to live up to it! Progress, not perfection, is the biggest cornerstone of the Chillpreneur philosophy: lots of tiny tweaks make change more achievable. My path to the Chillpreneur keyless life has come from a constant examination of what's *not working*. I regularly ask myself these important questions: 'What's feeling bad right now?' 'What do I want instead?'

I give myself permission to want what I want, and then I take action to eliminate, automate, or delegate the things I don't want. Nothing is too small! I mean, I didn't realize it would be life-changing to have electronic keypads on my door, compared to 20 seconds of inconvenience! When you systematically eliminate the things you don't want, you'll have more energy to create the pleasurable things you *do* want. It might take time, but incremental changes will lead you to an amazing and abundant place.

If you think of the opposite of the keyless life, it would probably be the *locked-in life* – one in which you feel trapped, annoyed, inconvenienced, restricted, and irritated. You might not even realize how much energy things take up in your life until you release them. It's like an old computer that doesn't have enough memory and is running too many programs at once – you don't realize how slow it's become until you get a new computer.

Establishing a keyless life for your business begins with choosing the business model that's right for you.

Types of Business Model

A few years ago, I won a business award and one of the runners-up (a guy) apparently said, 'I can't believe I lost to a *blog*!' Ha, ha! Yeah, you did.

The 'traditional' world of business can seem a lot more tangible than the entrepreneurial world does, and some of your friends and family might not quite understand what you do. You might even struggle to articulate it yourself. I used to try and explain, but now I just say I'm a writer (even though I barely consider myself one) and people seem to be happy with that explanation.

Seriously, just self-publish a book, so at Christmas you can tell Uncle Bob you're a writer, and your grandma can tell the same thing to her bingo friends instead of making it seem like you're involved in some dodgy online scam. There's no point trying to explain it! Of course, I'm not 'just' a writer either, but the point is that your business model doesn't have to be perfectly defined to be successful. There's going to be a lot of trial and error and experimentation (and failure), and it will shift and change over time as your desires and lifestyle change. That's the beauty of Chillpreneurship!

There are many traditional types of business model, but I'll simplify them into four main categories. There are pros and cons to each, but which one you choose will come down to your personality and what you like to do.

Maker Model

This entails making physical things – for example, clothing, toys, art, jewelry, and candles. You might consider yourself an artist, an artisan, a creative or designer. You might sell your wares to a distributor, wholesale to a larger company, or sell it yourself – either in person or online, on a site like Etsy. You generally have one-off sales or commissions, but many makers are branching out into subscription models, along the lines of the old Book of the Month club, but with new products like crystals, makeup, and crafts.

Lots of makers struggle to earn money, either because they underestimate their profit margins, don't charge enough, or buy into the 'starving artist' mentality. But that doesn't have to be your story! I often suggest that makers add other models into their business, and I'll show you how later in this chapter.

Service Model

This entails serving clients and solving problems for them, including 'done-for-you' work that delivers a tangible result. Examples include event planning, graphic design, editing, videography, photography, software development, being a virtual assistant, bookkeeping, etc. Your payment options might consist of one-off sales, packages that deliver a particular outcome, a retainer model, or an ongoing subscription.

A lot of entrepreneurs start out with one-to-one service models because they don't need a lot of set-up. You can literally just start helping people with nothing more than a computer (you definitely don't need a fancy website). Sure, it's an hours-for-dollars model and not very leveraged, but as long as you charge well, you can create a great living fast with very little lead time.

Consultant Model

Consultants help individuals, groups, or organizations through a transformation in a high- to medium-touch way. You don't necessarily do the work – the client is generally responsible for the outcome – but you use your processes, expertise, and tools to support the client. You might give specific advice or take people through a process using your expertise.

Examples include life or business coaches, health professionals, healers, advisors, astrologers, fashion consultants, interior designers, and mastermind leaders. You're paid for your personal time and expertise, either as one-off consultations, packages, or on a retainer.

Teacher Model

Teachers instruct groups of people in a low- to medium-touch way. Examples include authors, speakers, podcasters, online course providers, and bloggers. You're selling your expertise, advice, opinions, or entertainment value, and not necessarily your personal time one-on-one, so it's less hands-on than the consultant model. You can do this in person (at conferences or retreats) or online. Sources of revenue could include royalties, speaker fees, advertising revenue, and course fees.

Mixing and Matching Models

Your business might mix and match between models or have overlaps, which is totally okay. You might even change it over time as your lifestyle evolves (for example, if you grow your family, or decide to go traveling).

There's a fine line between the consultant and teacher models, but it mostly comes down to the depth of relationships. For example, I'm a teacher because I'm low-touch and very hands-off, and less of a consultant, who would develop deeper one-on-one relationships with clients. A lot of entrepreneurs adopt both models.

There's obviously an overlap between some of the models, and most entrepreneurs I meet work in more than one (or would like to). Here are some good examples of adding in other models to your business:

✤ Nicola Newman (née Chatham) is a fine artist who sells beautiful abstract paintings through galleries and does commissions for commercial buildings like casinos. As an artist, she's a maker. However, she has an online course teaching art (teacher) and co-runs a business mastermind (consultant). She's the perfect example of how a maker can also teach others while also consulting with other makers on subjects such as making their businesses more profitable. Best of all, she lives on a boat and travels with her husband and their dog!

✦ Karly Nimmo owns the voice-over agency Killer Kopy (a service); she started a podcasting school (teacher), branched into private podcast coaching (consultant), and also runs a business mastermind for women (also consultant).

✦ Jade McKenzie has an event management agency, Event Head, (a service), as well as a DIY course for entrepreneurs who want to run their own events (teacher), and offers one-on-one coaching sessions on all things event-related (consultant).

Why would someone teach a DIY version of their services, like Jade does? People are often worried about cannibalizing their own clients if they teach what they know, but it usually doesn't work out that way. They are two different target markets! Some people like to do it themselves, and others (like me) prefer to hire it out.

Either way, you're helping people with your expertise. Plus, adding a DIY course can serve two purposes: it sets up some passive income for you, so you don't have to take on every client (more on that later) and it actually gets you more clients because some wannabe DIYers realize it would be much easier to just hire you!

Again: you just have to find the right business model to suit your personality. As a major introvert, I love the teacher model because I can do it mostly online, and I don't have the patience to work with people one-on-one long-term in the consultant model. Even though I've dabbled in the service and maker models, I've found what works for me and my personality.

Choosing the Perfect Model for You

'If I'd observed all the rules, I'd never have got anywhere.'
MARILYN MONROE

The Chillpreneur solution to finding the perfect business model for you is: *Know thyself.* You might be saying, 'Wait, Denise, shouldn't I research the market, analyze my target customer, and design my business for what other people want? Isn't the customer always right?'

No, because you can offer only what you can offer. When you become clear on who you are, it will naturally help you be honest about who you can and cannot help. You don't have to serve everyone, and that's okay! It's not sustainable, and I know this contradicts most business books, but service doesn't have to be servile either. For example, if you love...

✤ **Constantly creating**... Consider offering a membership site through which you regularly offer low-cost content, books, or other products. You can charge a monthly or yearly fee and just keep adding more content to keep your members engaged. (This combines the maker and teacher models.) A lot of creators resist making money out of their talents and just end up giving away too much for free, for little return. If you're prolific, charge your community for it!

✤ **Forming deep relationships**... Consider creating a mastermind (a group coaching experience of like-minded people), so you can work with a small group of clients intensely over a specific period of time. (The consultant model.)

✤ **Facilitating deep relationships among other people**... Consider running group challenges or events during which participants achieve a huge transformation and support each other in the process, or create a business where you play 'matchmaker' for people or businesses. (This combines the service and teacher models.)

❖ **Sharing what you know, but not being responsible for people's results**... Create something that gives you short-term wins, like public speaking, writing books, being a guest on other people's programs; or use your 'celebrity' to promote other people's products and services. (This combines teaching and short-term consulting.)

❖ **Giving freely**... Consider establishing a 'freemium' offering – for example, a free Facebook group through which you make paid offers. (This combines the service, teacher, and consultant models.) Just make sure you have an offering because otherwise you'll stay in the free trap forever.

❖ **Working with high achievers**... Consider establishing VIP days or business retreats during which you work intensely with your clients for short bursts, with no ongoing commitment afterward. (The consultant model.)

❖ **Creating something, and then continuing to improve it**... Consider creating a single evergreen program and keep making it better each time you run it. (The teacher model.)

Exercise: Finding Your Model

In your journal or in a conversation with an entrepreneurial friend, answer the following questions:

• What's your primary business model?

• Does it work with your personality type?

• Is there a model you'd like to drop from your offerings?

• Would you like to add another model?

— CHAPTER 5 —

Are you Killing the Golden Goose?

> *'O Lord save us from overworking!*
> *Grant us grace to rest awhile.'*
>
> LAILAH GIFTY AKITA

You know the story of the Golden Goose, right? There are many variations on it, but my favorite goes like this:

A man had a goose that unexpectedly started laying a golden egg every day. It soon made him very rich, but he got greedy and impatient and wanted to become even richer. So, he cut open the goose to get all the golden eggs at once. But all he discovered inside was goose guts. There was no gold, and the man realized that, in his greed, he'd killed the source of his wealth.

There are many things Chillpreneurs can learn from this story, and the first is that *you* are the Golden Goose. You can profit for a long time through your skills and talents, but not if you kill the source of your creativity.

When Mark joined my business and saw what I'd created (a million-dollar turnover, despite my working part-time and half-assing everything), he concluded that, if we just worked harder, had more launches, and perfected everything, we'd make even *more* money! Let's flog that Golden Goose! Not only did that kill my energy and enthusiasm for the business, it almost killed our marriage! I'm being dramatic, but there was a lot of yelling and resentment during that first year of working together.

Without me, there is no business. Maybe I could squeeze a bit more profit, but for how long? It's taken some time, but I've learned to care for myself well enough to keep laying the golden eggs that my family relies on. I've become a fierce advocate and defender of my inner Golden Goose – protecting it from anyone who demands more than it can deliver (and sometimes that's me!)

Are You in Burnout Mode?

Many of my business friends have experienced burnout recently, and I have, too. I was almost ashamed to acknowledge it because it felt like admitting that I couldn't 'hack it,' which is a huge part of the problem. I was embarrassed that I was suddenly so 'weak,' and I beat myself up about losing my motivation for my business. In my quest to succeed, I'd created way too much work for myself, and one day I woke up feeling completely empty. I was burned out and just wanted to sit and play mindless games on my phone.

Look, I admit that I'm the kind of person who goes on holiday and still thinks about work. I'll get blog ideas during a relaxing massage, and I love going to my office and digging into work on Monday mornings. I'm a high achiever by any measure, and that's never going to stop. If that's you too, let's just accept that we're lifelong learners and consummate entrepreneurs. We're always thinking about our businesses because we love them. There's nothing wrong with that. But if that leads to burnout because you never take time off, or you resist sustainable business practices, it's a huge problem. And if you're not having that problem now, you will one day.

I often overestimate what I can achieve in a month, regularly schedule launches back-to-back, and forget that I'm a human who needs time off for pleasure and restoration. Ignore your body and your need for rest at your own peril. Do you really want to burn out in a few years' time, instead of having a long, successful, and rewarding career? Me neither.

> *'We need to do a better job of putting*
> *ourselves higher on our own "to do" list.'*
> Michelle Obama

If you have a business that requires every drop of blood, sweat, and tears, it's only a matter of time before it catches up with you – either in the form of a health wake-up call or another type of disaster. I've had friends who only stopped working because of a cancer diagnosis, the traumatic birth of a baby, or another 'forced intervention' from the universe. We can avoid that intervention by consciously choosing to look after ourselves first, and we often succeed a lot more quickly when we do. Remember: we're in this for the long term. You are the only finite resource in your business. Protect the Golden Goose and you'll be able to create abundance for a long time.

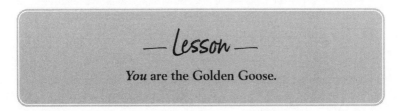

— *Lesson* —

You **are the Golden Goose.**

Three Ways to Kill the Golden Goose

There are three key ways you may be killing your Golden Goose right now:

1. Insisting on perfection

2. Working harder doesn't always work

3. Not knowing when to quit

Way #1: Insisting on Perfection

> *'When you're passionate about something, you want it to be all it can be. But in the endgame of life, I fundamentally believe the key to happiness is letting go of that idea of perfection.'*
>
> DEBRA MESSING

Being a perfectionist will cost you money. If I were having brain surgery, I'd obviously *prefer* my surgeon to be downright finicky about cleanliness, about making the perfect incisions in the right places, and being super-anal about my stitches. An engineer building a bridge *has* to be a perfectionist, but in business, it's not always the best trait, and your company probably doesn't need brain-surgeon-level perfection. Your perfectionism probably manifests as procrastination. It stops you from starting or finishing things, and it stops you from feeling proud about your accomplishments.

When Mark first came into the business, he started to critique everything. And to please him and his fresh eyes, I listened for a while. He said my webinar slides were unprofessional and my sales technique was too vague. He wasn't being mean: it's just that he thought we could do better. So I made sexy slides and produced slick videos. I hired a speaking coach so I could sell better from the stage. And guess what happened? Our sales went down! Plus, I felt like a big, fake *failure*. Finally, I said to him, 'Honey, people like my down-to-earth, imperfect style. And I love being genuinely detached about the sales process because somehow it works better!'

Even though it killed Mark to admit it, I was right. Yes, if it were his business, he'd always create the perfect, most informative slides. Yes, he would have followed a strict sales formula. But that's him, not me. He's a Boy Scout who loves following rules. I'm not, and it didn't work for me or my business.

Then I told him a story about Marilyn Monroe. Billy Wilder directed her twice, through notoriously tricky shoots on *The Seven Year Itch* and *Some Like It Hot*. Monroe sometimes forgot her lines or was too nervous to come out of her dressing room. Of course, the results were still magical and iconic. When asked why he put up with it, Wilder said: 'My Aunt Minnie would always be punctual and never hold up production, but who would pay to see my Aunt Minnie?'[1] Marilyn brought the magic.

I said to Mark: 'You would be able to run my business perfectly and way more professionally than me, but to be brutally honest, my peeps are showing up to see me, not you!' I had to accept my magic was enough for my audience. From then on, I dressed how I wanted to (tie-dyed dresses on stage, sometimes barefoot) and reverted to my casual, imperfect sales style; I felt much happier. People know pretty quickly if I'm not for them, but my personal integrity was much more important than currying their favor. And wouldn't you know it, sales increased again!

Look, I *know* perfectionism. I'm a Virgo and we practically invented it! If I'm not careful, I can beat myself up over everything in my business. Creating the perfect business plan, writing the perfect blog post, waiting until I have great hair and makeup before I get on camera, waiting to lose weight before I book my photographer, or scanning my horoscope to find the 'perfect' day to launch.

But I've also been able to create a very successful seven-figure business by training myself to let some things go. If I'd waited until everything in my business was perfect, I'd still be living in a tiny apartment and driving my old car with the roof that sagged around my ears.

'Success has nothing to do with perfection.'
MICHELLE OBAMA

Embracing imperfect action in your business will reap huge rewards for you. I'm not suggesting you half-ass everything, but you'd be surprised how successful you can be by just showing up.

The perfect example is marketing funnels. Most of my business is run on 'placeholder' marketing. As in: 'I think this is total crap (it's not), but I'll leave it up until I create the "perfect version."' Most of my placeholders are still there years later – making money *and* helping people. The funny thing is that my community doesn't think they're crap at all, and they're really grateful for the information.

Taking Imperfect Action

Let's put some real numbers in to show you what your perfectionism is costing you. My free 'Money Blocks' audio is several years old, and every few months I think I really should add better slides, organize it a bit better, or perfect my follow-up email sequences. But I never get around to it.

Meanwhile, 1 percent of all the people who listen to the recording sign up to do my Money Bootcamp, at $2,000 a pop. Now, 1 percent conversion doesn't sound like a lot of people, but as of today, 21,737 people have listened to that super-imperfect audio, and around 217 people joined my Money Bootcamp as a result. Conservatively speaking, that placeholder audio has made me $200,000 and has helped thousands of people, even though I judge it as not good enough.

Yes, I know how much you want things to be pretty and, above all, *perfect*, but in the absence of perfection, why not put up an imperfect placeholder? You can improve it as you go, but you can't incrementally improve on nothing. Do what you can with what you have right now: knowledge, skills, and budget. The right people will hear the right message, regardless of your insecurities and your wish that it was better.

Trust me: I've never judged anything I've created as 'done' or the best I can do because, honestly, I'll probably never be 100 percent happy anyway. Tell yourself: 'This is only temporary; I can fix it tomorrow, but today I'm taking imperfect action anyway.'

Would I secretly love to spend hours perfecting everything in my business? *Yes*, a thousand times yes. But, perfectionism is often in the eye of the beholder. Most of your clients wouldn't notice the difference between done and perfect – they need your help now! Holding off until you're 100 percent happy will delay the success of your business because that day will probably never come.

The first version of my Money Bootcamp was filmed at home with my iPad. The second was filmed in a hotel room using an inexpensive camera. It wasn't until I was a few years into the business that I created super-professional videos and high-end branding. Meanwhile, some of my biz friends are still waiting for the perfect idea or the motivation to get started. I've made millions just getting started and improving as I went.

EXERCISE: WHAT IS PERFECTIONISM COSTING ME?

In your journal or in a conversation with an entrepreneurial friend, answer these questions:

- Is my need for perfection delaying getting my product or service out to market?
- Will further tweaks *really* benefit my customers (or will they just give me an anal-retentive sense of satisfaction)?
- Although it's imperfect, could this (website, presentation, webinar, etc.) help people as it is now?

Most of the time, the answers are *yes, no, yes.*

Answering these questions can help you to get out of your own way, take action, and make more money in your business with less stress.

— *Lesson* —

People want your magic, not perfectionism.

Way #2: Working Harder Doesn't Always Work

'We think, mistakenly, that success is the result
of the amount of time we put in at work,
instead of the quality of time we put in.'

Arianna Huffington

One of my early business mentors, Fabienne Fredrickson, told me a mantra that she said completely changed her relationship to her business: 'I work half the time for twice as much money.' The first time I tried to say it, it came out backward: 'I work twice as hard for half the money.' Oops. Nope. Let the words soak in for a moment and then see how it feels to say out loud: 'I work half the time for twice as much money.' What comes up for you? Disbelief? Do you hear a voice in your head saying, 'That's cheating!' or 'That's impossible,' or 'But Denise... how?'

Beliefs like these are why I see women who are earning $25,000 a year stressing about how they can crack six figures, thinking, *I have to work* four *times harder?'* I did the same thing when I made $250,000. I couldn't do the math to figure out how to get to a million dollars. Surely I'd have to work harder, but there weren't enough hours in the day! I was already dangerously close to burnout, so four times as much work might actually *kill* me!

Here's the counterintuitive truth: you actually have to *work less* to earn more money. You have to work smarter not harder, and you have to master the lessons of discernment. You get to let people support you in your business, and you have to give up control over doing everything yourself. You have to embrace elimination, automation, and delegation.

Too much focus on effort can have the opposite effect – we can get bogged down in procrastination, over-complication, or resistance to delegating. But what if it were allowed to be easier? What if you could create your business in a way that worked perfectly for you, without feeling like you're paddling upstream? It's possible. It doesn't mean you'll never have to work; business isn't effort-*none* but it can be effort-*less*.

It's okay for you to make money with ease and flow. Honestly. Often people say to me, 'You must be so busy,' to which I respond, 'No, I'm not!' Honestly, you'd think I'd said something outrageous: it's just so taboo to admit you're not that busy. It's actually the b-word I say the least! The truth is that I work a lot, but I just don't feel *busy*. It's because every part of my business and life is set up to help me thrive. I don't do things I hate. I don't work with people who annoy me, and I rarely feel stressed. I make it look easy, but it took conscious effort to get here.

Now, let's talk about hustle. Let me be super-clear on this – my business didn't happen by accident. As I explained in the introduction, in the early years, I worked *a lot*. But that's not sustainable. I noticed how many entrepreneurial 'gurus' talk about how you have to 'grind' every day until you drop. But a lot of these people lead incredibly unbalanced lives. Some of them crash and burn or wreck their health/ marriages/businesses as a result of their hustle. They don't look healthy, and when you look behind the scenes of their businesses, some aren't even that successful.

If that's hustle, I want no part of it. I really like my sleep, and telling women to simply get up earlier – as if we don't have enough sleep deprivation in our lives already – isn't sustainable. I've seen some friends squeeze out all their energy for diminishing returns, or worse, serious health consequences. If you have kids, it's even harder to live that way. So please, don't feel like a loser if you can't figure out how those high-octane Insta-success-stories do it.

I personally don't want to live that way, and if you feel the same, I'm telling you there's an alternative: chustle (chilled hustle!) Just do the things that matter and leave everything else. If you want to make more money, you have a choice: work harder, or leverage everything in your life and make it easier.

> — *Lesson* —
> **It's counterintuitive, but you actually**
> **have to work less to earn more.**

Way #3: Not Knowing When to Quit

> *'Know the difference between a bad*
> *day, and a bad business.'*
>
> YVETTE LUCIANO

I was one of those kids who had a new business idea every month and roped my friends into doing things like collecting horse poop to sell (never got around to the actual selling, though). My twenties were the same, as I tried out dating coaching, real-estate sales training, multilevel marketing, and a very brief stint as a nude art model. I've never been short of a good idea. But just because something is a good business idea doesn't mean it's meant to be *your* business. Just because you *could* do it, doesn't mean you *should*; and just because something makes you money now doesn't mean it will work for you long term.

There's nothing wrong with experimenting. As an entrepreneur, you'll try lots of things (again, look at Sir Richard Branson), but a business is not a prison sentence. Just because you started something doesn't mean you have to keep that idea forever (even if your friends and family tease you for starting yet another business). Changing your mind isn't a waste of time and energy. Especially if you've realized that you're paddling upstream, no longer love what you're doing or, on reflection, realize that it's no longer your zone of genius. Stop digging a deeper hole and hand in your shovel.

You might think that because you've invested time, energy, or money, you're not allowed to change your mind and say no: 'But Denise, I just registered the best domain name!' You might have paid someone to create a website for your new idea and feel bad about spending that money with no results. (The psychological term for it is the 'sunk cost fallacy.') But what you've invested is never a waste. You can learn from any business 'failure.' The bigger waste would be to stick with something out of stubbornness or fear and never find your true calling. A bad business fit doesn't get better with time.

When you were younger, do you remember hearing things like, 'You made your bed, now lie in it' or 'Finish what you started'? These lessons applied to everything from emptying your plate (even when you hated what was on it) to finishing the roller-skating lessons you'd begged your parents for (even if you'd realized that skating wasn't for you). The message is that if you've screwed something up, you've got to live with the consequences *forever*.

My eldest daughter, Willow, once came home from school and announced: 'You get what you get, and you don't get upset,' which is something her schoolteachers said whenever kids whined about not having the specific crayon they wanted or didn't want to eat their lunch. The sentiment seems benign, even catchy (and I totally understand why the teachers say it), but I told Willow, 'Yes, but some things can be negotiated!'

In reality, you can renegotiate anything. You don't have to keep throwing good money after bad or investing your energy in something that no longer fits, even if it feels scary or irresponsible to change. Mark and I teach our kids to make deals with us. If they disagree with us, they have to use their negotiating skills and convince us otherwise. We want to teach them that their reality is totally up to them.

It's never too late to change your dream, tweak your business, or pivot in an entirely new direction. The idea is to continually shave away the 'don't wants,' so your life and business get closer to your ideal. This takes inner work and self-reflection, and the courage to change and negotiate every part of your reality.

Have you ever been to a Cher or Elton John concert? They both sing songs that are decades old and have probably made them millions of dollars. Do you think they get sick of them? Maybe they do, but they remind me that, if you're going to put a song out into the world, you'd better make sure it's one you *really* like!

What could you sing about for decades? Choose wisely. Money is a subject I've been able to be passionate about for a long time, and I'm beyond grateful that I gave up my early business ideas and am not *still* talking about weddings or toilet hooks. Nothing is wasted; you retain every skill you learn, and even your screw-ups can be invaluable lessons. Every 'practice' business is one step closer to your Chillpreneur one!

How do you know the right or 'perfect' business model to follow? You have to experiment and see what feels best, makes the right amount of money (which is not always necessarily the most money, if that feels horrible to you), and honors your energy. Let the rest go. It's okay. You don't have to do all the things.

Kill Your Darlings

In his book *On Writing: A Memoir of the Craft*, Stephen King (one of my favorite authors) writes, 'Kill your darlings, kill your darlings, even when it breaks your egocentric little scribbler's heart, kill your darlings.'

What does he mean by this? Author Ruthanne Reid says, 'Darlings, in writing, are those words, phrases, sentences, paragraphs, and even chapters that we are often most proud of. We love them, to the point that we *almost* don't care if those bits are clear to readers or not. We love them, and we want to keep them.'[2] The first version of this book contained almost 100,000 words, and I had to kill (delete) a lot of darlings!

In business, we have to 'kill' our darlings, too. When I started my personal development company, I tried to solve problems that I had no business addressing. My website had six different topics, each with a cute little tab; they were: goals and success, health and beauty, career and purpose, wealth and money, romance and love, and Law of Attraction. Even though I'd briefly run a soulmate course, coached a few clients on dating, and written *Get Hitched, Lucky Bitch*, helping people date was not my true calling. So, I eventually deleted it from my website. I was trying to be everything to everyone, and it diluted my real message.

Entrepreneurs often do this because they want to be inclusive, but also because they're afraid of turning down an income opportunity from the universe. Some people like working with generalists and others love specialists. I decided that I was going to market myself as a specialist, so, one by one, I killed my darlings until I talked only about money and mindset, which made my message much clearer to my audience.

My umbrella topic became helping women in business with their money mindset, and I decided to talk only about money mindset, which included money blocks, fears, and challenges; pricing, which included the mindset and psychology around what to charge, and how to charge; and money boundaries, which included dealing with problems and how to have awkward money conversations with clients. Everything else was now out of scope and it took discipline not to stray from that. It didn't feel restricted – it actually was a relief to have some parameters for myself – and my business grew more quickly because my audience wasn't confused every week about what I could offer them.

Should You Change Your Business?

Answer these questions:

❖ Are you completely bored with your topic?

❖ Do you feel like you've said everything you can say about it?

❖ Do you secretly hate or resent a lot of your clients?

'Yes' answers are a good sign that you're in the wrong business. It's okay to change.

One of my first 'serious businesses' was Raw Brides, which was about helping women lose weight for their wedding using raw food. Though it was kind of an interesting business model, it was honestly not me. I didn't like talking about weddings, I wasn't a weight-loss expert, and I wasn't a raw food expert. So, after about six months, I started losing steam because it wasn't enough to hold my attention. Ditto with my 'green detox queen' website and my movie review blog. I didn't make a penny out of either.

But what if you actually *do* make money out of a business you no longer love? Now, killing darlings takes courage when you rely on them for financial support. Sometimes you have to transition slowly; other times you need to rip off the bandage quickly and create a vacuum for new income streams. Giving up the old enables you to move forward and welcome the new. It's so empowering to let go. Not only does it free up a lot of time and energy, it creates space for new things to be birthed.

You're allowed to walk away from a business, even if it's a hugely successful one. Sarah Wilson, a former journalist and magazine editor, created a multimillion-dollar business out of a thyroid disease diagnosis. Personal research and experimentation led her to cut out refined sugars. She started writing about it, and that's when things snowballed. One sugar-free recipe book turned into numerous bestsellers and, inevitably, demand called for a course and an online community. One-and-a-half million people had completed her eight-week 'I Quit Sugar' course by the time she closed it in 2018 because the business wasn't working for her anymore. She was just… complete.

On the closure of the website, Sarah says, 'Seven years into a movement, five years into a business, I feel my work in the realm is done.' She considered selling the business but didn't want to compromise on quality or stay on for a transition period. She said, 'Success is a funny thing. It requires feeding. It requires growth. Which sees you become caught up in the cycle eventually, sometimes without realizing.'[3]

Even though the business was (wildly) successful financially, it had run its course. Even if she'd put the business on autopilot, there would still have been customer service to provide, a website to maintain, and it would still have demanded her energy. She was just *done*, and I respect the fact that she was true to herself and walked away from a successful business, even when people thought it was crazy. Sometimes the money just isn't worth it. You might not believe this if you're just starting out, especially when you're desperate to quit a job, but after a while, you'll realize that all money isn't necessarily *good* money.

How to Make the Change

Just do it. Don't feel like you have to be stuck with something just because you've built it. Making drastic changes can be scary, but they can also be liberating. Quitting a horrible job is an obvious step that requires courage. But tweaking – or even closing – an 'okay' or even really successful business can require courage as well. Changes don't have to be all-or-nothing. You could slowly ease out of the parts of the business that you hate and ease into a new direction. Or you could rip off the bandage in one fell swoop. It's up to you and your risk tolerance.

When I wanted to quit Raw Brides and start talking about personal development and money, I just emailed the people on my newsletter list and said, 'This is my new site, and this is what I'll be talking about from now on.' I didn't apologize, and I gave them the option to unsubscribe right away. There was no transition period – I just changed direction and it opened up everything for me.

You might lose some clients or money after making a change, but remember, when you do something that you love, you will actually make more money in the long run.

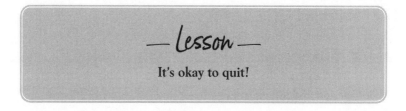

— *Lesson* —

It's okay to quit!

Tweak and Pivot

Now, you might be exactly on track, but chances are that your business could use a few tweaks. You don't have to throw the baby out with the bathwater: you could keep most of your business the way it is and just change a few things. For example, Cailen Ascher Marone, creator of the 3-Day Workweek Schedule, moved from coaching and teaching one-off courses to a membership model. She says, 'I'm a content creator and community leader at heart, so this shift feels much more aligned with my natural energy and talents.'

Ashley Stahl, founder of Cake Publishing, says, 'I moved from private coaching to e-courses, and back to private coaching after burning out on funnels and tweaking. I've gone high-end, and I've had a lot more joy in my work!'

Many entrepreneurs have a defining moment, such as burnout or the birth of a child, that necessitated change, but others realized that their business didn't bring them joy or enable them to work to their strengths. I once had someone ask me to buy her business, which, on the surface, was a fantastic fit because she taught people how to create passive income. I couldn't figure out why I was hesitating to make an offer, until it hit me: I don't teach how-to, I teach *mindset*. So, even though the topic was perfect, the method wasn't. It was a small distinction that had a huge impact on me: I tightened up the content on my blog to focus more clearly on mindset lessons rather than how-to stuff that could date.

You can keep a running list of things you want to stop doing, things you want to start doing more of, and boundaries you want to adjust. Here are some examples:

- ✤ **Stop doing**: this could be a service that you hate. A naturopath friend also offered massages in her clinic, but resented giving them because the work hurt her back and hands. As long as people kept booking, though, she figured she might as well earn money while she built her naturopathic practice. Sometimes you have to create a vacuum before the ideal clients come in, though. After months of moaning about it, she finally took the service off her website, and her naturopathy business exploded. Why? She'd created the mental and emotional space for something she loved better.

- ✤ **Start doing more of**: this means bringing more clients that you just click with into your business; or creating more time when you feel perfectly in the flow. Put more of those things into your business, and you'll thrive! Ask yourself how you can replicate the experience, either by seeking out that specific opportunity or by shifting your marketing to attract more of that particular type of client or project.

❖ **New boundaries**: this could simply mean a shift in the way you do business. A florist told me she hated doing weddings, but it was by far the most profitable part of her business. I asked her if she hated the work itself. 'No,' she said, 'but I find it overwhelming.' I asked if she could make it more enjoyable and worthwhile – for example, by increasing her prices. She decided to become a more premium business that took on fewer clients for more money. Now she's experimenting with new prices to see if she's in the wrong business or just not happy with how much she was being compensated for it.

Honestly, most of the time it's a money thing. You'd probably be happier if you earned more (we'll talk about this in Part III: Money). But that's not always true. For example, people often ask me to create a business mastermind, which is not my zone of genius and not something I can hold space for while our kids are young. No amount of money would actually tempt me to do it.

EXERCISE: TWEAKING YOUR BUSINESS MODEL

In your journal or in a conversation with an entrepreneurial friend, ask yourself these questions:

- What could I tweak in my business?
- If I had enough money, what would I ditch in my business?
- Have I outgrown parts of my business? Why am I holding on?
- Is the idea of quitting all or part of my business freaking me out? Why?

CHAPTER 6

Two of My Dumbest Business Mistakes

'You don't learn to walk by
following rules. You learn by
doing, and by falling over.'

RICHARD BRANSON

I've made a *few* business mistakes. Okay, more than a few. One big one was making physical products; a close second was creating a mobile app. Now, on the surface, neither looked like a screw-up, but internally, both decisions were wrong for me and were driven by various forms of procrastination, self-sabotage, and the fear of missing out. (By the way, if you make physical products or apps, I'm not dissing your business model. One person's keyless life is another's prison.)

Here are my two most recent mistakes (I'm sure they won't be the last), and some lessons that are applicable to any business.

Mistake #1: Making Physical Products

My path to physical products started out innocently enough: instead of business cards, I got fake money made with my face on it. It was fun and cute, and my community loved it. Then, when I started doing live events, I thought it was a *must* to give everyone a branded notebook, pen, and calculator. I almost made giant $50-note beach towels, but stopped myself just in time.

Then, during a spectacular procrastination session, I started making Lucky Bitch swag – for no reason (I didn't even sell it). Of course, I didn't get out my sewing machine or buy my own kiln – there are tons of companies who'll support your procrasti-branding by making things on demand; all you have to do is upload your logo and they'll ship it to you. For example, I made Lucky Bitch cushions, a towel, wrapping paper, Christmas ornaments, stickers, etc.

And *then* I found a site that does print-on-demand clothing. So, naturally, I made my own branded kimonos. Now, to be fair, they've come in handy because my staff can wear them to my events, but still... *kimonos*. The clothing company had a wealth of options, so I also made a hideous jumpsuit, a mesh tank top, a one-piece swimsuit, and a zippered clutch bag. I almost went for the yoga pants, but my accountant started questioning the validity of all my branded merch, and I had to cut myself off.

Just because the technology exists to make branded merchandise inexpensively, does not mean you should do it – *unless* it's your business model. My business is helping women release their money blocks, not making branded bikinis and Christmas ornaments. I'm a big advocate of fun marketing, and people regularly ask me where they can buy the branded Lucky Bitch merch. But the answer is: you can't. It's not my business, and I don't care if I could make a few bucks from it.

Beware Shiny Object Syndrome

Shiny objects are the sexy new ideas that prevent you from focusing. Before you go out of your primary offering, ask yourself: is this a valid business extension or a distracting sabotage? I admit that, now my business has been successful for a few years, I do sometimes get itchy or bored. Hence the branded mesh yoga tank top! I recently discovered a company that makes branded clocks. Could I make one with my popular mantra, 'It's your time, and you're ready for the next step'? Yessss – *no!*

For most entrepreneurs, the 'rush' of being in business comes at the beginning, during the startup and innovation phase. This is why you'll feel compelled to create a new website even when your current one is fine. Resist the urge. Seriously, get a hobby instead. Get a new haircut. Don't blow up your business just before things start working.

When you find yourself tempted by a shiny object, ask yourself whether you're procrastinating or whether it's a legitimate pivot in a better direction. Is it for credibility? Does it lead into more profitable work? There could be easier ways to achieve that. Beware of how your procrastination manifests itself. Whether it's collecting another certification (procrasti-learning) or starting a new business offering because your mentor (or business nemesis) does, get real about how it's impacting your income.

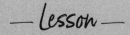

— *Lesson* —

There are easier ways to make money.

I should put that on a T-shirt and sell it! Wait... No!

Mistake #2: My Money App

Now let's talk about my money-tracking app. On the surface, it was a huge business win: my community loved it, and it's both gorgeous and useful. But I went into it for the wrong reasons. This is kind of embarrassing, but I literally made it because the author Danielle LaPorte had one. I didn't think about why I wanted one – it just seemed like the thing to do. It felt sexy, cutting edge and, on the surface, seemed to fit into my business.

I invested around $12,000 in design and development, and when it came to picking the sales price, I realized my big mistake. Apps are generally priced very cheaply, maybe a few dollars, and low-cost products don't fit into my business model. Oops! My philosophy is 'free or expensive.' I've deliberately built a business on giving away information for free and also leading people into my paid courses. Free means I can walk away at any time; free means that my freedom is my most important value.

I've also noticed that, when something is cheap, disgruntled customers feel even more entitled and angry when something goes wrong. So, rather than scrapping the app after investing all that money, we made it free. It feels generous, we don't have to deal with refunds, and if anyone has tech problems, we can apologize but don't have to spend endless hours trying to solve the problem.

I felt peace at that decision, but I drew the line at creating an Android version of the app. Almost every day, someone says '*Pleeeaaase*! I'll even pay for it,' or they straight-up demand I create it for them. My response is always, 'I'm really sorry, but I'm never making one.' Yes, it hurts to disappoint people, but I'm not going to throw good money after bad now I've realized my mistake. To be honest, I'll probably discontinue the app at some point to simplify my business even further. Even though it was a good idea *and* people liked it, I'm just not in the app business. Not everything has to be my business. What I offer is free or expensive. Lesson learned!

The 3 Percent Customer Service Rule

Wait, isn't it better to be paid *something* than nothing? Not really. Not all money is equal or fun to earn. Once you put a price on something, it comes with a certain set of customer service expectations. If I'm asking for money, I'd rather it be worth my while.

In my experience, at least 3 percent of customers need a lot of extra help, or in worst-case scenarios, become 'nightmare' clients. Unless you want to deal with that yourself, you'll have to hire someone to manage the inevitable emails and social media messages. People will lose their login or password details (sometimes more than once), have software glitches, need help figuring out how to access things, and want refunds that need to be processed.

This is true whether you're charging $2 or $2,000. If 1,000 people bought my app at $2, my revenue would be $2,000; and if 1,000 people bought my Money Bootcamp, my revenue would be more than $2,000,000. If 30 people needed significant customer service help in both scenarios (and were potentially annoying to deal with), which would *you* rather spend time on? Is it worth two bucks for me to deal with a disgruntled customer? Not really. That's not my model, and I'd rather have the two million bucks thanks very much!

Get Real About Your Return on Investment

It takes as much time (often less) to create a more expensive product as a cheap one. *Read that again.*

Think of books – it can take nine months or more to write and publish a book, and the average cover price is between $5 and $30; your cut will be just a few dollars. Creating my app took several months and it cost more to produce than most of my courses that sell for *a thousand times more.* What's the obvious choice? More or less work?

Everything you do in your business and life is an energetic trade-off. Think about the implications of expanding your business model. Does the change require more customer service, technical help, or physical work such as shipping? Again, if that's what you do, it's fine. But if not, it will distract you from your true work.

If my courses and the app each convert to sales at 1 percent (which is normal, as we'll discuss later), which would you rather create? My preference is always to go for the most profitable business that causes the least amount of hassle. That's when you become a Chillpreneur.

It's okay to say no. You don't have to be everything to everyone, even if it's a good idea. Your community wants live events, but you don't want to travel? Say no. Clients want you to get up at 5 a.m. for a coaching session in their time zone? Say no. People ask me to create a men's version of my book *Get Rich, Lucky Bitch*. What would I call it – *Get Rich, Lucky Dick?* Lucky Dude, Lucky Bastard? Sorry, no.

If you ask them, your audience will give you tons of random ideas, but you don't *have* to act on them if they don't fit with your values or your preferred business model. You don't have to do all the things for all the people!

— *Lesson* —

Not all ideas are good (for you). It's okay to follow the easiest and most profitable ones.

— CHAPTER 7 —

Five Essentials for a Chillpreneur Business

'Simplicity is the ultimate sophistication.'

CLARE BOOTHE LUCE

*W*hen my daughter Willow started swimming lessons, we'd take her into the pool with her inflatable armbands regularly for practice. One day, she lay back and said, 'Mama, floating is my kind of swimming.' So zen. At four.

That sweet girl teaches me so much about the Chillpreneur way. She doesn't expend energy without a good reason, always finds a shortcut, and she's constantly showing the rest of the family the art of relaxation – hence her nickname, 'Chillow.'

I'm not saying that every day in your business will be a picnic. There's still work to do, your comfort zone will be challenged, and you can't entirely escape the minutiae of life. But you can definitely make things easier for yourself. A true Chillpreneur business helps you create a lifestyle entirely on your own terms, which means you choose when, why, and how you work and – most importantly – how much money you make from it all.

In my experience, there are five things that make the most significant difference in creating a profitable lifestyle-driven business:

1. Get clear on your income goal.

2. Decide how you'd like to work.

3. Create passive income sources.

4. Build a support team.

5. Set up a home that helps you thrive in business.

Some of what follows might sound boring or complicated, but I'll show you how to set it up in the easiest way possible without getting stuck in perfectionism or analysis paralysis.

By the way, if your partner or parents are asking you for a business plan (because that's what they think will make the difference), we'll summarize everything with a three-page one later in this section. Having a sexy business plan means nothing – you're in business when you focus on getting clients and make some money. Money trumps planning any day!

Essential #1: Get Clear on Your Income Goal

> *'An average person with average talents and ambition and average education, can outstrip the most brilliant genius in our society, if that person has clear, focused goals.'*
>
> Mary Kay Ash

Author and entrepreneur Tim Ferriss teaches us that you don't need to be a millionaire to live like one, and many women don't want a big, complicated company or to sell their business to an investor. Success looks different to everyone, but it's hard to feel successful if you don't know what that means to you.

How much money would you like to make? It's a simple question, but often incredibly difficult for women to answer. Should you set a big stretch goal? Or be more realistic? Will you put out mixed messages to the universe if you change your income goal too often? For many women, picking a number can feel hard, and many entrepreneurs are scared to commit to a number for fear of doing it wrong or having only one shot at it. Setting goals and dreaming is free. Read that again: it doesn't cost you anything to do it. It's one of the most powerful manifesting tools there is, and yet we resist it for some reason.

Can you just wing it? Sure, you can. But setting an income goal will help you focus and can save you from shiny object syndrome. To build a Chillpreneur business, you have to know what you're working for. People often assume that I'm fantastic at setting goals or that I've cracked the 'perfect' goal-setting method. Nope. There isn't a single way to do it. How you set goals depends on you and your personality.

Don't procrastinate over setting an income goal to the point that you never do it. You're just picking a number, and it's not set in concrete – you can change it at any time. If you never set a goal, how will you know when you reach it? Some women hesitate to set it for fear of not achieving it, but what are the consequences? Literally nothing bad will happen to you!

'Goals are dreams with deadlines.'
DIANA SCHARF HUNT

Ways to Set Your Income Goal

A reference point can usually help you come up with a number. For example, your goal might be to earn:

1. More than you did last year

2. Enough to quit your day job

3. Enough to support your dream lifestyle

4. Enough to achieve financial freedom

It doesn't matter which goal you choose – just get specific about it and pick a number!

— *lesson* —

Setting goals is free.

Essential #2: Decide How You'd Like to Work

'If you don't like something, change it. If you
can't change it, change your attitude.'
MAYA ANGELOU

There are many paths to the same goal, and the Chillpreneur philosophy is about finding the one that works for you, your preferences, and your personality. You can set up your business in virtually any way you like. Challenge assumptions about how things are done in your industry and give yourself permission to break the rules.

Technology has given us much more freedom in how we deliver our work, too. Traditionally, face-to-face professions such as counseling, consulting, and healing have often been locally delivered, but they can now be conducted online, which many people prefer. I've had kinesiology, energetic healing, and psychic readings via video-conference. Most of my coaches, suppliers, and support people live on the other side of the planet, and it works out just fine. I've even had fashion consultations with stylists via email. If your clients don't like your method of doing business, they can work with someone else. There are no rules anymore. You can define any part of your business to suit yourself. Here are some things to think about:

How Many Hours Do You Want to Work?

Not how many hours you *think* you have to work, but what works for your lifestyle. When I first started out, I coached people six days a week from 5 a.m. to 9 p.m., depending on their preferences, not realizing that I could *choose*. My first action was to cut down the available hours, and then I gradually eliminated Mondays and Fridays from my coaching calendar.

Maybe you have kids and can work only a few hours a day. Perhaps you're a night owl. Guess what: you're allowed to choose! Nobody will create that for you; you need to decide for yourself.

How Much Human Interaction Do You Need?

Do you want to see clients face-to-face or serve them exclusively over the phone or internet? Do you want to sit at a desk all day, or do you *need* human interaction?

I love to work by myself. I've never liked collaborating with teams, at work or at university (group assignments were the worst!) My only exception is cohosting retreats with people I love, which I might do once a year. Other than that, I'm perfectly happy being alone.

Others miss the water-cooler life and interaction with coworkers. If you need people around you, then consider sharing a workspace, whether it's a coworking space, serviced offices, or a creative communal space. If you love being by yourself, make sure you designate a place that's yours alone and set it up so it's comfortable and you won't be disturbed. Neither way is right or wrong – it's just how you are.

In your journal or in a conversation with an entrepreneurial friend, answer the following questions:

- What has been my favorite working environment to date?
- How can I replicate it in my business?
- What do I need to thrive?
- What's not working for me in my current business?

Essential #3: Create Passive Income Sources

'No matter how good you have it, it's cool to want more.'
MINDY KALING

When I was starting out in business, I was utterly seduced by the concept of total passive income. The plan was to lie on a beach and do nothing while the millions rolled in. But I couldn't figure out a good idea, which is why my early entrepreneurial efforts failed. They were always about selling something I didn't really care about, so I could create the life I wanted *later*.

Then I realized that I'm a life-long entrepreneur. Even as I'm working on my 'early retirement' plan, I don't ever honestly want to retire. I'll probably be teaching, mentoring, speaking, and writing until the day I die, just like the incredible Louise Hay. But that doesn't mean *you* can't make things easier for yourself. Creating forms of passive (or leveraged) income means that you don't always have to spend your personal energy to make money. You can build in a buffer, so you don't have to take on every client, or so you can take time off when life stuff gets in the way.

What is Passive Income?

Investopedia defines passive income as 'earnings derived from a rental property, limited partnership or other enterprise in which a person is not actively involved.'[1] Of course, for entrepreneurs, there are many different forms of passive income. For example:

✤ Royalties from books/audiobooks (either self- or traditionally published).

✤ Income from an online course.

✤ Advertising or sponsorship revenue from a blog, podcast, or video.

✤ Income from affiliate marketing (promoting other people's products or services).

✤ Developing a mobile app.

✤ Licensing artwork or photography by itself or for products such as mugs or T-shirts.

✤ Drop-shipping other people's products.

First, some truth bombs from someone who has made millions in passive income. Ready? Creating passive income still requires work, sometimes *a lot* of work, at the start to set it up and keep it going. Doesn't that defeat the purpose? No. It's still a highly leveraged and mostly automated way to make money, but it's not entirely hands-off.

Why Is Passive Income So Awesome?

✤ **Money**. Duh. Making money while you sleep is fantastic.

✤ **Choice**. You don't have to say 'yes' to every client when you have other sources of income.

- ❖ **Energy**. Passive income conserves your energy – which you can then spend on things you prefer doing.

- ❖ **Impact**. You can help a lot more people without having to support each one personally.

My Sources of Passive Income

Let me share my own sources, and the work that goes into each one.

Books

Both my self- and traditionally published books require me to market them, including social media promotion and regular interviews. But luckily, I don't have to manufacture or distribute the books. My job is just to keep them top-of-mind for potential readers and update the content every few years. But the royalty money rolls in regularly, though it's just a small amount (a few dollars) per book sold.

E-Courses

I have several e-courses that sell on my website, don't require a lot of work, and are available to customers around the world, 24/7. However, the website still needs to be maintained, the content and brand need to be refreshed every few years, and, of course, there are customer service implications whenever you sell anything yourself. Still, this is so much easier than the one-on-one coaching I started out doing!

Affiliate Programs

I often promote other people's courses and get paid a commission in return. Although I don't have to create and fulfill the course I promote, there's quite a lot of logistical work involved in marketing and developing the affiliate relationship. This is an incredibly leveraged form of income, but it doesn't happen by itself.

Money Bootcamp

I created this course in 2012 and have since taught thousands of students. Although people can join at any time, I still have to launch and market it several times a year and spend time and money facilitating an online support group. This course, however, has helped me create millions of dollars in revenue, and I can outsource a lot of the logistics.

Passive Income Still Takes Work (at First)

Now, it might be disappointing for you to hear these truths about passive income, because it's tempting to think you can do nothing and still make millions. In my experience, that's not the case! However, here's some good news: it's not as hard as the alternative. Honestly, the hardest part is going to be overcoming the blocks you have to making easier money. For example, it may feel greedy to make money without working for it. Or it may feel like cheating.

When I started my business, it was very much an hours-for-dollars model. Coach someone; earn money. In that model, you're constantly looking for new clients. At some point, you'll hit an income ceiling with either your pricing or ability to take on more clients. So, I decided to take what I coach and teach it in small-group programs. Initially, my courses had five participants. But that grew to 20, then 40, and then hundreds of people. The workload was mostly the same, especially the set-up and selling effort, but suddenly, I was paid a lot more money per hour.

Then something fascinating happened. I started feeling guilty about making more money for doing mostly the same or less work. I launched my first e-book and, every time someone bought it (for 10 bucks), I felt incredibly guilty, like I hadn't earned it properly or I was ripping people off by charging for something I'd already created. I honestly felt like I had to call each purchaser and read the book to them over the phone to 'earn' that 10 bucks. I felt so bad that I stopped promoting my books and courses. They became incredibly hard to find on my website, and I knew I had broken links to the sales page.

All my life, I'd been hearing about this thing called passive income, so why was I sabotaging it? I'll tell you over and over again in this book: your money blocks will come into play in virtually every area of your business. Money blocks aren't the most important thing you need to overcome: they're the *only* thing. You're not an idiot. You can figure out how to write and publish an e-book, and you can research the steps for creating an e-course; it's not rocket science, but if you're still not doing it, why not?

Because you have an underlying belief that you have to work hard to earn money. It doesn't feel like an equal exchange if someone gives you money for something you no longer have to sweat over. Making passive income goes directly against that mentality, and that's why you resist it.

I had to get honest with myself: if I didn't need to pull all-nighters, stopped waking up at 5 a.m. to coach clients, or stopped hustling to make money, did I really earn it with integrity? Was I disrespecting the women in my family who had to work to make money – like my mother, who cleaned houses or worked long shifts in a nursing home? Who was I to have this easy life? If you're reading this and thinking, *What is she talking about? I love making easy money!* you can skip this section. But if you suspect that you're holding yourself back, read on.

Again, I'll be honest. Creating passive income requires a lot of groundwork at the beginning, and this is where most people get stuck. You have to build the vehicle (i.e., write the book or make the course), set up the technical systems to sell it, and create some form of marketing to let people know about it. All that stuff is easy(ish), and certainly achievable. But before you set about creating sources of passive income, you have to acknowledge your mental and energetic resistance.

Why Are You Resisting Passive Income?

Get honest and ask yourself these questions:

✦ What would happen if I was incredibly successful without burning myself out?

✦ What would I do without constant work and stress?

✦ What if my business was easy and profitable?

And then give yourself permission to go to the dark side and think about the potential negative consequences of that. Here are mine:

✦ If I'm too successful, I wouldn't be considered friendly or down-to-earth anymore.

✦ If making money is too easy, I'll lose my ambition and become lazy.

✦ I'll feel so guilty about my family being stuck in their jobs, that I'll have to give them all my money.

Patricia Lohan, a feng shui consultant, had massive blocks around making money from affiliate income, even though she was a natural and enthusiastic recommender. She told me, 'My yoga teacher's classes got sold out because I told everyone about her. Same with my energy healer and business coach. But every time they asked what they could do to thank me, I froze.'

Patricia's number-one value is connection, and for her, receiving money for her natural talent felt like she was sullying her relationships by monetizing them. She had to remind herself that she would never recommend anything if she didn't 100 percent believe in it, and that it was okay to receive in return. At first, she allowed herself to receive referrals in return, literally forcing herself to say 'You're welcome, and if you hear of anyone who needs feng shui, please send them my way!' Eventually, she was able to become a successful affiliate marketer and actually receive cash in return for recommending things she would have anyway.

What about you? What are your blocks for receiving passive income? Do you have excuses like, 'I don't know anything!' 'Nobody will pay me for *that*!' or 'It sounds too hard!' Let's talk about how to get started, and I'll show you that these excuses are BS.

What Should Your Passive Income Product Be?

Many women overlook potentially lucrative business opportunities because they feel too easy or obvious. You might think, *Why would anyone pay me for that?* But just because it's easy and enjoyable for you, it doesn't mean it's easy and enjoyable for someone else. There are a lot of things you take for granted that other people need to know. You can package that knowledge in various forms (a book, a course, an audio) and solve a problem for someone.

I've bought products that tell me how to get a baby to sleep (because I was dying from sleep deprivation), how to groom my eyebrows into a perfect shape, and how to create a month's worth of freezer meals (including done-for-you shopping lists). People (like me) are busy and/or lazy. Package things up for them, create extra value (like shopping lists to save them time), and make it easy for them to buy, even if they can find the same information online for free.

Sometimes customers have a desperate need for information and want a solution that works for *them* and their specific situation *right now* – like how to get their six-month-old breast-fed baby to sleep – rather than generic information that applies to everyone.

Start Small, But Start

Even if your topic has been covered a million times, think about how you can create something especially for an underserved niche of a market. Your first passive income product might be a 10-page e-book or five-minute audio. In fact, I recommend going small rather than spending a ton of time and money creating a big, complicated course or mobile app that you're not even sure people will buy. It means you can test out the topic. You don't have to get complicated with videos or confuse yourself with the tech requirements. And, if you have a small marketing list, it's a great way to get wins on the board and feel confident enough to go bigger next time.

Start sooner rather than later. You don't need to be The Expert of All Experts to start, and you don't need to create something that's perfect. The beauty is that you can always update and refresh your content. Perfectionists rarely create passive income, because they're always waiting, waiting, waiting for the perfect time, idea, or product.

My first passive income product was so basic: a $50 manifesting course that I filmed using my iPad. It wasn't sexy or professional, but my audience loved the information I taught. For me, creating that course was life-changing. Waking up thinking, *I made $50 while I slept* was a *huge* mental breakthrough for my abundance. If you do it once, you'll get addicted. A Chillpreneur doesn't have to hustle for every dollar. It's okay to make money-solving problems for people while you sleep!

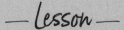

— *lesson* —

You're allowed to make money, even when it's easy.

Go With What You Know

You don't have to be the guru of all gurus and teach absolutely everything. Teach something you know – it might not be obvious to others. Don't teach people how to create a six-figure business if you've never done it, because you'll feel like a fraud (and rightly so). Teach what *you know* you know, even if you think it's too basic. You'd be surprised what other people struggle with.

Write a list of everything you've done in the last couple of years that you could teach to somebody else. And remember, it can be very simple because people are looking for basic information (think how successful the *for Dummies* books are). It's best to capture that now, while it's still fresh in your mind. Don't be a knowledge hoarder! Help others and make money.

EXERCISE: WHAT CAN I OFFER?

In your journal or in a conversation with an entrepreneurial friend, answer these questions:

- Is there something I've mastered that my friends always ask me for advice about?
- Do I have a unique method or system that I use in my business or life?
- What resources have I already created for myself that others would love?
- What's really obvious to me, but hard for others?
- What is my spin on an established topic?

Essential #4: Build a Support Team

> *'On the six-figure path, seeking support is not an option, but a requirement.'*
>
> BARBARA STANNY

Remember how I told my friend James Wedmore that I bet I could get to six figures on my own? What's so great about doing everything yourself? This is one case where rebellion is not a good business strategy.

Did you ever wish you had a clone to do your dirty work for you? You can! You've heard of the A-Team; well, part of running a Chillpreneur business is building a C-Team: your clone or Chillpreneur team. It's about taking the pressure off yourself to be the Chief Everything Officer.

Amber McCue, founder of the course 'How to Clone Yourself' and CEO School gives us a wake-up call: 'Self-made millionaires and billionaires outsource nine out of 10 times when there's someone else out there who can do it better. Other people tend to try to DIY everything – that's just not an efficient use of time.'[2]

Are your fears around outsourcing and delegating holding you back from making more money in your business? Almost definitely. Entrepreneurs resist building a team for many reasons:

✦ They don't want to manage a lot of people.

✦ They're worried about the investment.

✦ They feel guilty about delegating.

✦ They have a money block around working hard, and if someone else helps them, it doesn't 'count' or feels like cheating.

How do you feel about managing a big team? Do you think it's the only way to be mega-successful? Let me reassure you: I *hate* leading people, and I've always deliberately created a small, lean team for that exact reason; I reached the million-dollar revenue mark with just me, one part-time assistant, and a few key contractors.

My attitude toward hiring is always to follow the 'eliminate, automate, and *then* delegate' model. If I can eliminate tasks that nobody should be doing, then great. I'd rather automate tasks with software than add another person who I have to manage. If all else fails, I'll hire someone, but rarely on a full-time basis. And I usually hire a contractor to batch a bunch of tasks for me, so they aren't an ongoing employee.

It's hard to be chill when you're doing everything yourself, and it's hard to be a leader when you're wearing so many hats. It's okay for you to focus on the things you like. Hiring people isn't just nice to do – it's often a symbolic action that opens up much more abundance for you. When you've added payroll expenses, it will force you to value your own time more and focus on income-producing activities (the things people actually pay you for). When tasks are someone else's official job, they get done. My newsletter came out sporadically and sometimes not at all when I was responsible for it, but when I finally outsourced it to my assistant, it went out like clockwork every single week.

Put it this way: you can't be both the show pony and the plow horse in your business. You have to choose. When Mark came into the business, I realized that he works way harder than I want to. He finds it really hard to switch off, and he loooves giving me tasks. Recently I said to him, 'Babe, you have to stop treating me like a plow horse – I'm a thoroughbred.' As in: you can't keep working me in the fields all day. You have to rest me. Use me for the best and most prestigious events. Let me have time off to groom my coat... I mean, go to the hair salon. Feed and water me well.

If I have to work all day and night, I'm not only cranky, I don't work at my best. Mark wanted me to be 'on stage' and be the face of the business, but he also wanted me to do everything behind the scenes, including plowing the damned field. And I'd had enough. That's when I fully embraced the concept of hiring the right team. I got really clear on what my job was: showing up on camera and on stage and being the face of the business. Everything else could be outsourced.

Are you trying to be both the show pony and the plow horse? That's fine at the beginning, when you're the 'Chief Everything Officer,' but at some point in your business, you have to embrace the fact that even if you *can* do everything yourself, you shouldn't. You might not be ready for that yet, but you have to start somewhere.

Getting Started with Outsourcing

Chris Ducker, author of *Virtual Freedom: How to Work with Virtual Staff to Buy More Time, Become More Productive and Build Your Dream Business*, is an incredible resource for figuring out tasks to outsource. Google his '101 tasks to outsource to a virtual assistant' for some ideas. He suggests that you start with a simple exercise called 'Three Lists to Freedom,' which involves listing things you hate doing, struggle to do, or shouldn't be doing at all. For example:

Things You Hate Doing

You might hate bookkeeping, customer service, scheduling clients, or sending out your newsletter. When you hate something, you'll probably delay taking action, get essential details wrong, or take *forever* to complete even simple tasks. Bogging yourself down with things that stress you out isn't just part of being in business – it's a self-imposed purgatory. It's okay to find someone else who might *love* tackling those tasks. How awesome would it feel to take that off your plate?

One of the things I hate in business is dealing with email. It caused me so much angst that it bled into other areas of my life, and I'd think about the emails 24/7. I once heard a speaker say that if you're thinking or worrying about someone other than your loved ones at 3 a.m., then it's time to make a change and put boundaries in place with your clients.

I started outsourcing email to my first assistant, which took just five hours a week of her time. It didn't break the bank, but it saved me *hours* of time, not to mention the mental clutter. It paid for itself a million times over because I became much more focused on income-producing activities. Life's too short, and your energy too finite, to spend it on things you hate. *Say it with me: this is not the best use of my time.*

Things You Struggle to Do

When you're starting out, almost everything is a struggle! I spent many long nights Googling how to do something technical on my self-made website and wanting to tear my hair out. And yes, there's satisfaction in finally mastering something, but not everything is worthy of struggle! Someone else could do it much more quickly than you. Your time is valuable, so find the path of least resistance and don't waste your energy on things you're just not great at.

Get honest about your weaknesses. For example, many entrepreneurs are great at starting things but *terrible* at finishing them (um, me). I had a friend whose online course just needed some graphic design tweaks, but she kept procrastinating about getting it to launch date because it wasn't perfect. For some weird reason, she felt like she had to do it herself, and every month, she was losing potential sales.

If you're struggling to finish something because it's not in your zone of genius, outsource it to someone who is a completer/finisher. Don't beat yourself up over it or think you 'should' learn how to do it. That's not what you were put on this planet to do when someone else could do it for you. This could be a Facebook ads specialist, a launch manager, or someone to help you finish a project. Maybe you just need to hire a techy person to hook up your payment systems, so you can start receiving money. Whatever it is – stop using a lack of money as an excuse not to outsource things you struggle with. Sometimes you have to step forward in faith first, and invest in yourself so you can allow the money to flow easily.

— *Lesson* —

You can't be good at everything, and that's okay.

Things You Shouldn't Be Doing

In the early days, I did my own graphic design, and frankly, it was terrible. I had no business doing it and it impacted my sales. When I outsourced it to a (cheapish) designer, my business expanded because customers weren't turned off by my amateur brand anymore.

Get honest: what do you need to give up? It could be doing your own customer service or trying to fix a broken website. Hire people to do those things so you can more easily attract new clients or take orders. Be clear about what's an income-producing activity and what you're doing because you're being cheap or feel like you 'should'. *Not everything is your responsibility.*

Tips for Outsourcing

✦ **Start small**. This isn't all-or-nothing: *none* of the people you delegate tasks to have to be full-time, but it's essential to have the right people doing the right things. Every person you outsource to must move you toward your ultimate goal. None of the people you outsource to have to be ongoing, either. With an assistant, it's okay to pay for just a few hours each week, taking tasks off your plate that stress you out. And you can hire most other team members (graphic designers, copywriters, video editors, marketing strategists, etc.) on a project-by-project basis.

Stop thinking that hiring people is a big, dramatic, official commitment for life. The key is to figure out what's going to make *your* life as easy as possible and what's most in line with your personality. When I hire people, I see how we can make it a short-term, high-intensity project. For example, hiring someone to create a year's worth of social media content in one go, instead of spreading it over the year.

♦ **Progress, not perfection**. The truth is that you'll probably suck the first time you hire someone, and I really did (the first four times). It takes *practice* to delegate clearly, to give direction and feedback without feeling like a bitch. And just because you screw it up doesn't mean you're supposed to take the task on yourself again. It just means you're normal!

♦ **Care less about perfection**. The secret to delegating is to care a little less about how other people do things. This was the hardest lesson for me to learn as a perfectionist. 'Careless' is usually taken to mean not being thorough, or being negligent, but when I looked up the word again, one of the older definitions was 'free from anxiety.' Aaah, doesn't that feel good? So, instead of beating yourself up all the time, why not just care a little *less* about being perfect?

I find decision-making pretty tricky because I second-guess myself all the time. But now that I've embraced outsourcing and delegating, I've learned to be okay with things not being 100 percent perfect. It's honestly saved my sanity, and the results are frankly the same – if not better – than if I'd agonized over every little thing myself.

The trick is to hire experts and let them do the hard work for you. When you're starting out, you don't really see the cost-benefit, but trust me, having someone on your payroll will make you more conscious about creating sales. When you're more established, the cost savings will be obvious. Sometimes that's saving you scouring through information to find the best answer for you – other times you're borrowing their years of expertise to get a better result.

Does being a control freak about every little thing give you or your clients the best results? Not always. Done is better than perfect. Care a little less, and you'll gain a lot more peace of mind, *plus* your business will grow more quickly.

— lesson —

**It's okay to focus on what you're good
at and outsource the rest.**

Find Your Chillpreneur Team

The most straightforward approach is to ask people you know, advertise in your own newsletter, or post in your business networking group. Don't overcomplicate this. The biggest hurdle is overcoming your resistance. It helps to list all the reasons why you *shouldn't* have help, before you even start the process: 'I can't afford it' or 'I don't know what to outsource first', or 'I'm not good at delegating.' Frankly, these are all BS excuses. Remember – you can't afford not to, you can start small, and nobody is good at delegating at first. Try it out.

My biggest tip: don't hire people like you – hire for your skill gaps and weaknesses instead. I screwed this up in the beginning because I wrote job descriptions that sounded exciting to me, regardless of the role, and so I always hired Mini-Me types who were fun to interview. Guess what? When I was working for other people, I'd get bored after six months, get a new business idea, and quit my job. That's exactly what happened with my employees because I hired people like me. Entrepreneurs like me make shitty employees!

> *'The smartest thing I ever did was to hire my weakness.'*
> SARA BLAKELY

Being clear about your weaknesses will pretty much write the job description for you! If you read it and think 'yuck,' then you're probably on the right track to finding someone to complement your skill set perfectly! Give yourself permission: you don't have to do everything yourself. It's okay to have a Chillpreneur business in which you focus on doing the things you like. Start with the tiniest thing and go from there. And give yourself permission to screw it up a few times! It's part of the journey.

EXERCISE: GET DELEGATING

In your journal or in a conversation with an entrepreneurial friend, answer these questions:

- In my business, what's causing me the most stress right now?
- Who can I find to get this task off my plate?
- What's my biggest weakness in business?
- What would my 'dream team' look like?
- What's my biggest excuse for not delegating?

Remember: CEO doesn't mean Chief Everything Officer.

Essential #5:
A Home That Helps You Thrive in Business

In terms of a keyless life, I've really nailed it in my home life, and I actually spend more money there than in the business. I don't have to think about annoying things like changing the toilet paper or picking up mail. My laundry fairies always deliver nice clean clothes into my drawers, and my bedsheets and towels are changed weekly without any effort on my part. My housekeeper makes me snacks, goes to the post office, or calls the handyman if something breaks. I very rarely cook, yet somehow breakfast, lunch, and dinner appear on the table each day.

Basically, I live like a 1950s dad, and I love it! My life is set up for two things: maximum quality time with my family and maximum freedom for my work. I'm not 'too good' to clean my own toilet, but nobody will pay me to do it, so it's not worth spending my limited time or energy when I can outsource it. Women are taught that it's noble to do housework for their own family but shameful, lazy, and exploitative to pay others to do it. Have you noticed that nobody judges men who live this way?

I consider my home team as important as my business team because it gives me the freedom and mental space to do my work. I outsource every boring, mundane, or unpaid task that I can think of, so I can show up and serve my family and my community in ways that are important to me. My kids don't need to see me cook and clean to teach them how – they'll figure it out when they move out of home (I'll encourage them to split the cost of a cleaner with their roommates!)

Now, you might think the way I run my house is too extreme (or expensive) for you. But not so. Like anything, you can start small and upgrade as your income improves. But you have to start.

The 'When I Earn More' Myth

Many women cite lack of childcare as the most significant stressor holding them back from being successful in their business. So, why not invest in daycare or an in-home nanny (even for just a few hours a week)?

I often hear, 'My husband said that when my business earns more, we can pay for childcare.' This is the ultimate chicken and egg situation, but let me be clear: it's going to be hard for you to gain traction in your business if you never invest any time in it. The day will never come unless you're willing to get up at 4 a.m., and that's not sustainable or advisable. Sleep is really, really important.

Maybe you get childcare for just a few hours a week or your partner spends a couple hours with the kids after work every day – or spends the day with them every Saturday. Childcare isn't just your responsibility, and it's virtually impossible to combine work and kids at the same time. It's not fair to your kids, yourself, or your business. On the few occasions I've tried working while caring for the kids, it's made me want to tear my hair out, and one of them will ultimately tell Mark, 'Mama said the F-word a lot today!'

A Clean House Doesn't Grow Your Business

Every hour you spend on your business (especially if you focus on income-producing activities or on creating passive income sources) will positively impact the lives of your family members for years to come. The time you invest will exponentially increase your happiness and sense of power.

Housework isn't your sole responsibility either – even if you're not the main breadwinner right now. If your partner doesn't agree to pay for a cleaner until your business earns more, it's time for your house to get a little dirtier.

> *'I've seen women insist on cleaning everything*
> *in the house before they could sit down to*
> *write… and you know it's a funny thing about*
> *housecleaning… it never comes to an end.'*
>
> CLARISSA PINKOLA ESTÉS

I had a house cleaner way before we could afford it. I got sick of fights every Saturday morning about who would clean the bathroom, so we paid for two hours every two weeks, and it was life-changing for our relationship and my fledgling business. It never costs as much as you think to outsource a task like that (please pay your cleaners well), but it's priceless in terms of what it can free up for your time and energy. If your spouse complains, remind him or her of the phrase *Happy wife, happy life.*

If you're single, no one pays you to clean your toilet, either. It's much more lucrative to spend that time on your business instead. Get a cleaner every few weeks, hire a local person to run errands for you, or invest in a local meal delivery service so you actually remember to eat. Even if you're low on cash right now, getting a cleaner is a straightforward (and honestly cost-effective) way to take some clutter off your plate and help you focus your time on making *money*. This is especially important if you work from home. You shouldn't be procrasti-cleaning during the day (even if you think it's cathartic or meditative – seriously, there's better therapy than cleaning).

If I had to tell you the two things you should outsource first, it would be a cleaner and someone to tackle your email inbox. Neither will break the bank but will free up so much energy for you. Start small, as your budget allows, and don't feel guilty about it – you're building an asset that will pay for itself eventually.

Think of the Opportunity Costs

Outsourcing home tasks is highly symbolic because it means your time is worth something. Even before you have a lot of clients, the opportunity cost is too high to spend your time doing small, inexpensive (and frankly energy-sucking) jobs. Instead of cleaning your bathroom, you need to be out there getting your next client.

Working from home doesn't automatically mean you're the housekeeper. You are *working*. Even if you're starting out, you need to have dedicated time and space to grow your business. It's an investment in the future for your family. My hubby used to try to guilt me into picking up his dry cleaning during the day, and it required some serious boundary talks. Instead of saying yes or no, I'd simply reply, 'I'm at work, sorry – go on your lunch break.' After a while, he understood that my time was just as valuable as his, but I had to train him with that simple repetition.

Because I said no at the start, when my business wasn't yet earning much money, our family is now *hugely* abundant. That didn't happen because I picked up dry cleaning instead of working: it happened because of my *business*.

Outsourcing some household tasks will pay dividends in the future. It's excellent practice in asking for what you want, gives you valuable lessons around boundaries and creating standards for your business, and creates a job for someone else.

In my business, we now have pretty regular standards of how things get done, so I don't have to think about it. For example, the newsletter goes out at the same time every week, and it also gets turned into a podcast, transcript, and audio on the blog. It gets shared on Instagram, Facebook, Twitter, and in my private Facebook groups. None of that just 'happens' – I had to ask for it. And it's the same in your household. If your family is used to life happening by magic because you do it all, it's time for a change. Not because you're lazy or entitled, but because you have a bigger vision for you and your family. And you need to create space for that!

So, what would you like to outsource: cleaning, errands, cooking, laundry, childcare, gardening, maintenance, food shopping? Again, just pick one thing that will free up some energy. You have permission to create an easy life for yourself, so you can focus on growing your business.

EXERCISE: OUTSOURCING AT HOME

In your journal or in a conversation with an entrepreneurial friend, answer these questions:

- What stresses me out the most at home?
- What stops me from working on my business?
- What would make me feel taken care of?
- What's on my dream outsourcing list?

Your Simple Business Plan

This was a big section, and now we're going to put it all together and create a simple business plan to keep you on track. Don't overthink it. Tiny tweaks and baby steps over time really add up. You can download a template for the plan at Chillpreneur.com/Bonus and fill it out.

Set Your Income Goal

How much money would you like to make?

✤ More than you did last year?

✤ Enough to quit your day job?

✤ Enough to support your dream lifestyle?

✤ Enough to achieve financial freedom?

Pick one of the above to come up with a number and set your income goal.

My income goal: ....

Decide How You'd Like to Work

✤ How many hours do you want to work?

✤ Are you selling the right thing now?

✤ What method of business works best for you?

Create Passive Income Sources

Start small with what you know, and list your top three ideas for a passive income product.

1: ....

2: ....

3: ....

Build a Support Team

Decide on the three things you want to outsource first by identifying what:

✤ You hate doing

✤ You struggle to do

✤ You shouldn't you be doing at all

Set Up a Home That Helps You Thrive at Work (and Vice Versa)

✤ What stresses you out most at home?

✤ What stops you from working on your business?

✤ What would make you feel taken care of?

✤ What's on your dream outsourcing list?

Get Accountable

Create a now/next/later list that summarizes all the actions you'll take, like the one opposite. Try not to put everything in the 'now' list (I see you). You can recreate this table in your journal or download a template for it at Chillpreneur.com/Bonus.

	Now (urgent)	Next (3–6 months)	Later (6–12 months)
What can you eliminate?			
What can you automate?			
What can you delegate?			

💡 The Big Idea

If you remember nothing else from Part II, remember this: You *are the goose that lays the golden eggs. Set your business and home life up in a way that ensures you'll keep laying them for a long, long time.*

— PART III —

Money

INTRODUCTION

Money

'Making money and doing good in the world are not mutually exclusive.'

ARIANNA HUFFINGTON

I saw memes floating around on social media for a while asking, *Would you stay in a haunted house for a year for $100,000?* Hundreds of people had commented on them, saying 'Sign me up!'

Why, though? You don't have to *suffer* to make money. You don't have to do things that are scary, against your values, or cause problems in your life. It's totally okay for you to make money doing things you love!

Why are we in business? To help others and to make money. It's straightforward. If you don't help enough people, you won't have a sustainable business. And without the money part, all you have is a hobby – sometimes a very expensive one! Helping people probably comes very naturally to you. In fact, you've probably done it all your life. Women tend to be great at the helping part and not so great at the money-making part. That's where I can help.

Here's some Denise real-talk: if you can support yourself, you should. Many people don't have the opportunity, ability, energy, or capacity to do it, so if you can create a ripple of abundance for yourself and others through your success, why not? We live in a time of great opportunity – use your privilege and create financial independence for yourself and your family. There are no good excuses, so don't let money fears hold you back from starting or growing your business. Claim your worth, support yourself, and use your money to do good in the world.

In this part of the book, I'm going to take you through the trickiest thing women face in business: *money!* We're going to talk about setting and increasing your prices, where and when you should *never* work for free, and how to deal with awkward conversations about money (you're going to have *plenty* of those).

Let's get started!

— CHAPTER 8 —

Big Pricing Mistakes

*'If you undervalue what you do, the
world undervalues who you are.'*

SUZE ORMAN

A simple question that's often difficult for business owners to answer is: 'So, how much does it cost?' When asked that yourself, do you stammer, or deflect the question? I have, many times! Now that I'm on the other side of it, I get impatient when a business owner clearly doesn't want to tell me how much something costs. Please, just tell me the price so I can pay it! It's annoying!

When I was a fledgling life coach, I was just as clueless about pricing as everyone else. I'd never had to think about it before – all of my previous jobs either had fixed day rates set by my boss or were an internal cost to the company. I didn't like having salary conversations and *never* asked for a raise or bonus. I took what I was offered (like a good girl) and never thought I was worth more.

When I decided to go into self-employment as a full-time life coach, it was suddenly *my* responsibility to assign a monetary value to my skills, and that was scary. Too expensive would make it look as if I was too big for my britches, too cheap and I'd look inexperienced. I wished someone would just *tell* me what to charge.

In working with thousands of women over the years, I've seen pricing patterns emerge among the mistakes they make and believe me, I've made them all too! Knowledge is power, though, and if you can recognize these mistakes when they arise, they'll be less likely to derail you. In this chapter, we'll look at the *big* pricing mistakes I've seen, namely:

1. Pricing by committee

2. Undercharging and over-delivering

3. Working for free for too long

4. Taking 'you're too expensive' personally

Mistake #1: Pricing by Committee

The worst thing you can do is ask other people what they think you should charge. It's an innocent mistake: as women, we think we're being inclusive, collaborative, and harnessing the wisdom of others by asking them for their opinion. But it's a dangerous practice.

Here's why: every time you set your prices by committee, you're taking on other people's beliefs around money, regardless of their qualifications, experience, or money mindset. Imagine that your money blocks are physical things – like rocks – and you have to carry them around in a backpack. Obviously, the more money blocks you have, the harder you have to work just to go about your daily life. When you crowdsource your pricing, you're not just carrying *your* backpack of money blocks, you're taking on everyone else's too!

Not all feedback is useful. If you don't believe me, try it yourself. Go to your favorite business forum and ask a pricing question. You'll be astounded by the variety of responses. Everyone has a different perspective on 'worth' and 'value.' Before you pay any attention to what others say, ask yourself the following questions.

Are They My Target Market?

Taking advice from people who are nowhere near your target market – for example, your husband, uncle, or a random stranger – is a big mistake. I remember talking to a 50-something guy about my business at a networking event and on hearing what I did, he said, 'Wow. It sounds like you're charging *too much*.' I felt chastised and embarrassed because he was reflecting my own worst fears about my business. 'Yeah,' I said, 'I think you're right.'

This dude was the complete *opposite* of my target market, but I let his opinion sway one of my most important business decisions. His view of my pricing could have been based on what his own target market could afford, or on something more sinister, like an ingrained misogynistic view of what women are worth.

Either way, it was totally useless, but the interaction played on my mind for days. He wasn't my coach, and he wasn't a pricing or marketing expert. He knew nothing about my business or target market. He just made a snap decision based on what he 'felt' was too expensive, and I believed him!

His opinion was none of my business, so why was I soliciting it? Why even have this money conversation with some random stranger? Honestly? Because I didn't want to think about it: I wanted someone else to *tell me* what to charge so I didn't have to confront my fears about money. I thought someone else would know better than me.

> *'… if you're just looking to your friend, co-worker, husband or wife for validation, be careful. It can stop a lot of multimillion-dollar ideas in their tracks in the beginning.'*
> SARA BLAKELY, FOUNDER OF SPANX

If you have a specific niche (and you definitely should), then how tightly do the people offering their opinions fit that profile? For example: age, gender, geographical location, income level, stage of life, or business. If your ideal target market is parents with a healthy income, why would you take the opinion of a childless senior citizen, or vice versa? It doesn't make sense!

If you market to other business people, what stage of business are they in? What's appropriate for a beginner to pay is entirely different from someone who's financially successful in business. Nobody knows more about your business than you do. Nobody knows your target market's hopes and dreams as well as you do. And nobody is more deeply and emotionally connected to your business goals than you are.

Another question to ask yourself is:

Are They in The Market For What I Do?

Until people actually need something, they don't really know what they'd pay for it. My Goddess, when I think of what I've paid for things, either because I needed them ASAP, or because I got excited about the results I was promised. It must be hundreds of thousands of dollars by now! If you'd asked me what that product or service was worth beforehand, I probably would have vastly underestimated what I would've paid.

My budget is way more flexible than someone starting out in business and, to be honest, my time is worth more now, so I'm willing to pay to outsource to an expert. I've always appreciated paying for professionals in my business – for example, copywriters to help me with sales emails. But I never considered paying a ton of money for copywriting until I needed to create 35 scripts in two weeks for a new course I was filming. I procrastinated over it until I had no choice, and ended up paying four times my budget because I was suddenly in the market and needed it done ASAP! It was totally worth it, even though I had unrealistic expectations about what I should pay beforehand.

So, unless the people giving you advice represent your target market *and* need you now, they won't give you accurate or useful advice. If you need a ballpark figure, a better question to ask your business buddies would be *What do you do, and how much have you paid for X?* For example, 'If you've been in business for at least two years, what did you pay for your website?' or 'Hey, health coaches, what did you pay for your website photography?' That way, you're getting advice from people who have put some money in the game, and it's useful market research rather than confusing random opinions.

Asking Competitors or Peers

What about other people in your industry? Should you ask them or sneak a look at their prices and place yourself accordingly? Again, this isn't even remotely helpful. You might believe that the seniority (or popularity) of your peers means you can't charge as much as or more than they do. Maybe you're judging yourself against the 'popular girls' in your industry and think that social media follows mean superior experience?

At the start of my business I decided that I didn't deserve to charge as much or more than established coaches who were decades older than me, regardless of their skill level. Now, that sounds reasonable on the surface, but I was discounting my years of adjacent coaching and mentoring experience, of which I had plenty – both in jobs and as a volunteer. In my own mind, that didn't 'count,' and I told myself I needed to start at the bottom of the ladder.

However, longevity doesn't always mean you're great at your job. I know lots of 'experienced' coaches whose skills have been stagnant for years and, frankly, aren't that great. Maybe you know those types too? Plus, look at professions like social media management – a long career in that field isn't even possible since technology changes so quickly. In a case like that, results and knowledge are just as valuable as experience.

Lastly, your industry might have massive money blocks (the alternative healing professions come to mind). So remember, when you're averaging out the competition, you're basing your income potential on collective insecurities and industry myths. Money coach Kendall Summerhawk says it best: 'Don't base your net-worth on someone else's self-worth.'

If you can't survey your audience (or a rando guy on the street), and you can't sneak a look at what your competitors are charging, *what's a Chillpreneur to do?* The simple answer is: you have to trust in your own wisdom and set your own prices. Nobody is going to do that for you. Just pick a price and try it out. The truth is that what you charge is entirely personal and not as black and white as you'd think. You're looking for the 'Goldilocks sweet spot,' which is the 'just right' price for you, regardless of what other people charge.

Author Danielle LaPorte calls this being 'comfortable in your money shoes.' It has to be the right fit. Too big price-wise and you'll feel like a fraud, like you're a little girl playing dress-up in your mama's high heels. But wearing too-tight money shoes that you've outgrown (prices that are too small) is incredibly uncomfortable too. You have to feel as if you're in alignment and in integrity with your rates, and only you can decide what that is for your business. Sorry!

— *Lesson* —

Stop comparing your prices with other people's, or soliciting unqualified feedback from unqualified people.

Mistake #2: Undercharging and Over-Delivering

'All underearners, without question, share one common trait: a high tolerance for low pay.'

BARBARA STANNY

Ah, what a classic combination! Often, if a woman finds charging difficult, when she finally does accept money, she'll feel compelled to over-give to the point where she might not make much money at all. And even then, she'll feel guilty!

I've done this often. Picture this: I was on stage leading a free workshop, and it was time for the 'upsell.' This is my least preferred way of selling, and I hate it, so I always overcompensate with the bonuses. My offer was a one-day live workshop, teaching all my secrets of manifesting success, for $97. I'd undercharged in the first place, but then, in my desperation to offer value, I also threw in two 60-minute, face-to-face coaching sessions. A crazy, awesome bargain, right? But I wasn't done: 'If you decide today, you also get these bonus earrings.' Yes, *earrings*.

In my defense, they were cool earrings with 'Love' written on them, and one of my manifesting tips is to wear affirmation jewelry, but it was a completely unnecessary bonus. The $97 offer was good enough as it was! Women came up and threw cash at me for the workshop, and why wouldn't they? I was practically giving away the naming rights to my first-born child! Hey, why don't I come over to your house and clean your toilet while I'm at it? Cook you dinner? It was like a bad infomercial. But wait, there's *more*!

Of course, once I added up all the expenses for the event, the cost of all those in-person bonus coaching sessions (parking, coffee, and the hassle of putting on a bra), *plus* those stupid earrings, I wasn't making much money at all, certainly not for all that effort.

And that, my friend, is the *huge* mistake a lot of women make around pricing: being over-generous to the point of self-sabotage. Maybe we do it because we don't believe we're worth it without all the bribes, bells, and whistles. We want people to like us, and we desperately want to help people make changes in their lives. Here's the thing: *What you offer is already amazing and life-changing.* Read that again. Let it sink in. Your work can stand alone without making you broke, or making you resent your clients. Plus, you're allowed to make lots of juicy profit!

Almost every time I create a new product or event, I fight the urge to over-deliver. We usually think it's a good thing to give our clients more, but it's not. A course stuffed to the gills with extra information becomes incredibly overwhelming and failure-inducing. I know this because I looked into why refund requests were creeping in for my Money Bootcamp. It turned out we had too many modules and too much bonus material. People thought they had to complete it all and felt like failures before they'd even started. When we reduced the amount of content, the refund requests went down. Less really is more!

Over-giving can disempower your clients. For that reason, I don't recommend *ever* offering bonuses like unlimited email coaching if you're a service professional (it's a pain in the butt that really doesn't teach your clients self-reliance or boundaries). And I don't recommend adding premium services like face-to-face coaching unless you're charging appropriately for it (your personal attention should always be your most expensive offering). Over-giving can also be terrible for the environment. Branded stress balls and endless USB flash drives end up in landfill or clutter up your office. Don't add to the problem!

The same goes for over-delivering in terms of time. Humans need time to integrate and apply information, so if you're a coach and you're having monster three-hour sessions with your clients, you're probably overwhelming them with information, most of which they'll forget almost instantly. When we try to jam our years of experience and knowledge into one session, it's often incredibly tiring and uncomfortable for our clients. Then they don't rebook because they want to implement everything from the last session (which is impossible). So, over-delivering can ultimately derail your client. Again, less is more.

Are You Undercharging?

> *'Profit is not an event. It's a habit.'*
>
> MIKE MICHALOWICZ

Guess what? Not only are you allowed to charge what you're worth, you're also allowed to make a healthy profit. *Say what?!*

I once bought a beautiful handmade soapstone jewelry box from a local bookshop for $14. *Fourteen dollars.* I said to the owner, 'I think these are underpriced. It's clear that a lot of love goes into them.' He replied: 'I know – my wife does an amazing job, but we'd rather be affordable for people.'

First up, 'affordable' is different for everyone, right? Those soapstone boxes would still be a bargain at $25. Plus, handmade items *should* be more expensive than mass-produced ones, and many people are happy to pay a premium for something that's made by an actual human being. I hate to think how little profit they are making on those boxes, especially when factoring in the woman's time (which I suspect they aren't doing). It's a shame, because I bet she'll give up, get discouraged, and lose her enthusiasm for the craft pretty quickly.

My first-ever business was selling handmade bracelets made of wetsuit remnants. I bought the raw materials for two dollars and sold each bracelet for... two dollars. Okay, I was nine, but still. The thing is: I loved having a business. I loved creating, and I even loved selling. It didn't occur to me that I could make money too!

Women often feel guilty about making a good profit, especially on something that feels good, is easy for them, or is something that helps transform people's lives. But that's the whole point of being a Chillpreneur: it's *supposed* to be easy and feel good. So, make sure you're adding up all the true costs of doing business – including your time and expertise – and make sure you're *actually* making a profit! If you're not, you have to increase your prices.

You're even allowed to pay yourself a salary! I know, *crazy*, right?! Paying yourself is incredibly symbolic. Why? Because most of us will move heaven and earth to pay our suppliers and make sure they are taken care of. In fact, I've been so stressed about not being able to pay an invoice on time that I went after more sales or chased down clients who defaulted on invoices I sent to *them*. I hate letting other people down.

But guess who comes last? Who works her ass off? Who does the buck stop with? You. You deserve to get paid, and not with the leftover scraps. There will never be any 'spare' money left over for you until you stop undercharging in the first place. Charging appropriately is an act of self-care and self-love. It's not greedy or unethical to charge well for what you do. Money is a tool that helps women take care of their own needs and use their energy and resources to help others.

You might think you're doing people a favor by undercharging, but it rarely works out. It can lead to burnout and resentment, and you won't have the energy and vitality you need to make a difference in the world. So, stop being cheap with yourself – it serves very few people, least of all you. *You are enough.* You might not believe that, yet, because it's so deeply ingrained. But you are.

— *Lesson* —

**You don't need to bribe people to work with you.
And you're allowed to make a healthy profit.**

Mistake #3: Working for Free for Too Long

'Time is money.'

BENJAMIN FRANKLIN

One of the most symbolic milestones of your business journey is graduating from free to paid work. For many, it feels like a leap too far, which is why otherwise talented entrepreneurs get stuck in their day jobs for way too long.

I very deliberately use the word 'graduating' when it comes to charging for your work, because it should be a natural progression, like moving on from an unpaid internship into an actual paid job. Real-talk: graduating from being a moonlighter (or hobbyist) to a full-time entrepreneur requires you to actually charge people money!

At some point, you just have to decide that you're ready and that, even if you never believe you're good enough, you're going to move forward. The Chillpreneur way is realizing that your imperfection is perfect. Because you'll never feel ready, have enough testimonials, feel validated enough, or be free of doubts about whether you're good enough. That's the inner work you need to do, not the actual hard work and hustle.

Now, there's a difference between working for free and intentional volunteer work. It's healthy and generous to build some philanthropy into your business, whether you're giving time or money. But know the difference. Philanthropy usually feels good and has no other motive than giving back. If you're being exploited, you'll feel out of alignment.

> *'To be in business you must generate a profit;*
> *otherwise, it's called volunteering.'*
>
> SUSAN W. ANTAL

Reasons to Work for Free

Beyond philanthropy, you might decide to work for free strategically, and there's nothing wrong with that. Valid reasons include the following:

- **To gain valuable experience**. Maybe you're working toward a certification and need to log client hours. Or you need testimonials for your website, test cases for your portfolio, or case studies for your blog. In that case, working for free is the quickest way to achieve your goal. It's totally fine: get 'em booked ASAP! Just decide in advance how many clients you'll take on for experience purposes and cap it at that. You don't need to live in apprentice mode forever. You're allowed to earn while you learn.

- **To promote your work**. Most businesses can find a way to let customers 'try before they buy.' For example, if you've got a course, you can give away some lessons for free and finish with, 'If you liked this, here's where you can buy the full version.' Don't forget to make the payment link really obvious: you don't want to make people work to give you money.

- **As a sales strategy**. People understandably want to see if there's an energy fit before they commit to working with you, so doing a small (emphasis on *small*) amount of work for free can be an awesome sales strategy. A lot of different service-based businesses can do this. You could offer 'mini makeovers' for a web page (not the whole website), a free critique of a sales page, or copywriting feedback. This isn't working for free, and you have to be clear that it's a taster or trial to see if working together is a win-win.

- **To gain exposure to your target market**. I do several interviews on podcasts each week, just to get in front of my target market. It's totally a win-win situation. However, nowadays I'm more selective about what I say yes to. It has to be a good fit, and it has to be a sizable audience. I've done my apprenticeship and have been interviewed for a blog with five followers, but I've since graduated to blogs with a bigger reach. When you're starting out, say yes to almost every opportunity for the experience, and then become more discerning as you go on. You'll figure out what to say no to over time.

What About Speaking for Free?

I get asked to speak for free all the time – not just at events in my hometown, but in different states and countries – by organizers with zero budget. Some think that 'there's no harm in asking,' just in case I happen to be in their neighborhood on the other side of the world at the exact time and date of their event. Um, no thank you. There's a 100 percent chance I'm going to decline that 'opportunity.'

Back in the blissful, carefree days before I had kids, I traveled the world attending conferences all the time, so it was no big deal if I spoke at an event I would have paid to attend anyway. Why not? After I had kids, I started adding up the true cost of speaking for free. Most conference organizers booked the cheapest flight available, so I had to pay extra to check in a bag or have more legroom, and they didn't always pay for a taxi to the venue. You'd be surprised how many organizers don't provide food for speakers, so there are meals, snacks, and beverages to pay for. There are also internet costs at the hotel, plus tipping everyone from waiters to bellboys to taxi drivers.

To feel confident enough to perform well, I need to look my best, so I usually have my hair and nails done. And, now that I have kids, there's the additional cost of childcare and the indirect cost of being away from my family. Like many mothers, I feel obligated to make up that time with Mark and the kids when I return. Then there's prep time. All the 'brain power' invested in speaking for free comes at the cost of developing my own income-producing assets. As an introvert, I also have to factor in recovery time. Putting on a bra and Spanx to leave my house and be in a room full of hundreds of people can wipe me out for hours and sometimes days at a time!

> *'If you don't value your time, neither will others.*
> *Stop giving away your time and talents. Value*
> *what you know and start charging for it.'*
> KIM GARST

Let's face it though: it's wonderful to occasionally sleep through the night without my kids waking me up, or use a hotel room to write or take a quiet bath. But get honest with yourself and calculate your costs: *all of them.* Then you can decide if it's worth doing. Sometimes it is! Sometimes speaking for free is worth it if the audience is your target market and if enough potential clients are there to make it worthwhile.

Don't get guilted into speaking for free just because it's a good cause or you feel like you should. Appearance activist Carly Findlay often gets asked to speak for charities, to provide disability awareness to organizations, and ironically, to participate on panels to promote equality and women's empowerment. All for free.

After being asked to speak at a career day for disabled students at a for-profit educational institute (another irony), she wrote on her blog: 'No doubt they'd pay a consultant specializing in an area outside of disability. No doubt the person running the event gets paid. For me, it'd mean an afternoon away from my day job, plus several hours preparing the presentation.'[1]

When Carly said no, the organizer said she was disappointed (ouch, the D-word always stings), and that she should have been 'happy to donate her time' because it was a worthy cause. Carly says, 'I believe the work that people like me and (other disability activists) do in educating people is important in facilitating change and improving access and inclusion, and it deserves compensation. Our work is not to be given away for free.'[2]

— *Lesson* —

**Be intentional about your free work and
calculate what it actually costs you.**

Melanie Ramiro, one of my Money Bootcampers (and someone I hired to coach me on speaking), advises having a personal quota for free events – say one per quarter. When you've fulfilled that, it's okay to say, 'Sorry, I've reached my quota for pro-bono work this year.'

Before You Work for Free

Many women have a seemingly unlimited capacity for giving, and they feel greedy if they expect something in return. If this sounds like you, here are some tips that will help you 'check yourself before you wreck yourself.'

+ **Put clear boundaries around your giving**. If you're giving away a certain amount of coaching or consulting hours, or designing a small website for someone, put it in writing, and when it's done, it's done. If you're speaking for free, don't feel obligated to stay for the whole event. One keynote and you're off the clock. Don't feel like you should market the event for free, either – that can be part of your paid speaking package.

+ **Be clear about the expected reciprocity**. If you're doing free work in exchange for something, i.e. a testimonial, professional pictures, or video footage, make sure you follow up and actually get it. You'd be surprised how often people overlook this because they don't want to nag or bother others, even when they agreed to it up front.

+ **Make it worthwhile**. If you do pro-bono work, let the recipient know what your rate is going forward, and make an offer for further work. If you're a speaker, can you sell books or products at the back of the room? Can you use the time to meet up with some paying clients around the event?

+ **It's always okay to say 'No, thank you.'** Working for free isn't bad in itself: just make sure you're doing it intentionally and for strategic reasons – not because you feel bad about charging.

Mistake #4: Taking 'You're Too Expensive' Personally

'If you think it's expensive to hire a professional to do the job, wait until you hire an amateur.'

PAUL NEAL 'RED' ADAIR

A tenet of the Chillpreneur philosophy is to 'take nothing personally.' You have to give up the illusion that there's a perfect price and that you can avoid criticism when you find it. *You can't please everyone.*

It feels horrible when you have the perfect solution for a client but they tell you flat-out that they can't afford it. That's when women feel shame around their pricing, decide they're being too greedy, and give discounts or concessions to fit into the client's budget. But 'expensive' is a relative term: something that one person sees as obscenely expensive can seem dirt-cheap to someone else.

Nowadays, I'm much more chill about hearing someone say I'm too expensive because I know I'm just out of their budget at that *particular moment*. It also might mean they *can* afford it but just don't want to spend the money. Or that I need to do some work on my sales page to better showcase my value.

You'll have people say no to your very reasonable quote because they 'can't afford it' and then see them spend money on something totally ridiculous the next week. It's not your business what people value or spend money on, and you don't have to change your pricing to meet their financial expectations. It's just a mismatch of budget, money mindset, or values – not a moral failing on your part. Your pricing is not a literal translation of your value as a human being. Money is just money. A price is just a price.

Having said that, yes, you can price too high. That might sound weird coming from a money mindset mentor, but I don't want to BS you. For example: you can price too high for your ideal client. If you've consciously chosen a target market that's on a low or fixed income, your prospective clients probably won't have the money to pay premium rates. So, it's a trade-off. A lot of women confuse their business with their charitable giving because they want so much to help a particular type of person. There's nothing wrong with that. But you have to be the right match price-wise with your target client, and you must have the right business model to support it.

You can also set your price too high for your client's business level. I don't often recommend that brand-new entrepreneurs work with super-high-end coaches because they're rarely in a place to get immediate value for their money. For example, I've seen newbies get flustered when they receive advice about how to up-level their business or create high-end branding when they don't even have the basics in place. It's okay to work with someone in line with where you're at.

I once invested $7,000 for an intimate group business day with a high-end coach. Half the room thought it was worth the money, and the other half felt like it was a big rip-off. What was the difference? Half were six-figure business owners and the rest had million-dollar businesses. We all heard the same advice, but it was mostly applicable to the million-dollar half of the room. Not because we were smarter (far from it), but because at that point in our business journey, the advice we received was more useful to us and had a quicker return on investment. We got the same information, we paid the same price, but we experienced completely different value.

> *'How you perceive yourself is how
> others will perceive you, too.'*
> Lorie Greiner

Understanding Pricing Psychology

What do you think when someone is 'cheap'? Remember, cheap is relative: what you consider cheap might feel expensive to someone else and vice versa. When people's prices seem too low, we often think they're just starting out or are inexperienced in business: I know I do. Are you giving that perception with your current prices? Do they make you look like a beginner? Or someone who is insecure about her worth?

When people charge too little, it doesn't automatically mean they're inexperienced or bad at what they do, but it makes me second-guess working with them because I'm suspicious of their price and the value I'll get in return, especially when I know that it often indicates unresolved money blocks.

In my experience, that causes problems for me – like the supplier who is slow to invoice (even when asked repeatedly), they will often over-deliver in a way that's not always useful (which can take longer to complete the original work) or be timid in taking charge because they aren't in their true power. I can feel their money 'stuff' leaking into every interaction and it makes me feel uncomfortable, or even as if I should coach them, when what I want is for them to take care of *me*.

As someone with money to spend, I want to work with people who have clean and clear money boundaries, and who don't buy into a power dynamic just because I earn more money than they do. I'm coming to them because of their expertise and how they can help *me*, not so I can help *them*. Quite simply: I like working with people who have worked on their money blocks! That doesn't mean they are perfect, but I can tell the difference.

Whether you're just starting out or an established professional, you don't want to offer the cheapest services in your industry. If clients say 'You're so cheap!' or refer others to you by emphasizing your low prices, take it as a sign that people have a different perception than you do around your worth. It's not necessarily a compliment!

As I said, I get suspicious when something is too cheap. It's like, what's the catch? With low-cost flights it often means a horrible seat on an old plane or a big layover. It's usually cheap for a reason. Now, let's look at the flip side. What do you think when you see someone with 'expensive' pricing? *She must be really good and worth the money!* I'm not saying this is true or fair, but that it's the reality of pricing psychology. A higher price often gives the perception of experience, mastery, skill, confidence, and higher self-worth.

Here's another reaction to high pricing: *That's not for me.* Does it feel unfair, exploitative, or exclusionary? Pricing yourself out of someone's budget or comfort zone doesn't make you greedy. It's okay for those people to be served by someone else. And it's okay that some people have to save up to work with you.

Do you remember wanting something that was financially out of your reach? You felt a sense of accomplishment when you could finally afford it. Why rob potential clients of the sense of triumph they might feel when they can work with you? I'm definitely not advocating price gouging. Most women can tell the difference between knowing their worth and being flat-out evil.

In 2015, former hedge fund manager Martin Shkreli bought the rights to an important HIV drug called Daraprim through his company Turing Pharmaceuticals. It used to cost patients $13.50 per pill, but he raised the price to $750 for no apparent reason other than wanting to make more money.[3]

Nobody thinks that's okay. Nobody cheered him on with, 'Go, girl, charge what you're worth!' Let's face it: Shkreli is a giant turd-burger. He was sentenced to seven years in jail for unrelated financial fraud, but you could say that karma got him. Shitty, unethical people are usually shitty and unethical in *all* areas of their lives.

That's not you. It's not evil or manipulative to make a significant living from your business – not only to put food on the table for your kids, but also to have enough money to live an extraordinary life. Because, unlike greedy dudes such as Shkreli, I know you'll do great things with your wealth.

Remember, there's no magical critic-proof price, which is why the Goldilocks sweet spot pricing method is so personal. Even if you undercharge, someone will ask why you're not serving clients for free

– guaranteed! Don't be offended; it's just a business rite of passage. People will ask you to lower your prices, no matter how low they are already, and it's okay to say no. I've heard this so many times. An entrepreneur agonizes over the price and finally quotes what she thinks is a low but reasonable proposal and the response is 'too expensive.' Those people aren't your customers.

One of my Money Bootcampers, Ingrid Tuffin, got an email from a prospective client saying, 'We have received your proposal. Your price seems high for this job. Would you like to amend your quote?' She wrote back simply saying, 'No.' We cheered her on! Make sure you're surrounding yourself with people who believe in charging what they're worth, otherwise, you'll constantly second-guess yourself.

Every time I've set my prices, I've had completely opposite reactions to the same amount. On the same day I've heard 'That's too expensive,' and 'Wow, that's great value!' Who would you rather serve? I'm not saying you can just sell a bag of horse poo for $10,000. But, if you're giving good results for $10,000, and it's appropriate for someone to pay that because they'll get a great return on that investment, charge the ten grand. *With pride.* Then wait for somebody to say, 'Oh, is that all? What a bargain!'

That's the truth about pricing. There will always be someone who thinks it's too expensive, and there will always be someone who thinks it's a great deal. You're not required to serve everyone, and many aren't going to be a match for your services or pricing. You don't have to convince them. You won't get your pricing exactly right the first or the 100th time. So, try not to worry about what other people say or think. Chill out and just pick a price.

— *Lesson* —

It's okay to be expensive for some people.

— CHAPTER 9 —

How to Increase Your Prices Without Losing Clients

'Price is what you pay. Value is what you get.'
WARREN BUFFET

If you want to earn more in your business (and you're not ready to add passive income sources), you have two main ways to accomplish it: work with more people or charge more. You may have already done the math and realized that you can't work harder without going into burnout and overwhelm. If that's the case, raising your prices is probably the easiest way to earn more money.

But you're going to resist it like crazy. One of the things women do – even after they get over the initial hurdle of setting their prices in the first place – is rarely review or change those prices. If that's true for you, you're either going to love this chapter or want to run away from it screaming.

I once mock-chastised my *very talented* photographer friend Claire Thomasina because I felt her prices were too low. She said: 'Denise, last year I was doing this practically for *free* – you've inspired me to increase my prices, but I need to sit here for a while before I jump again.' That's fine. Claire knew she was probably still undercharging, but she needed to acclimatize to her new rates before she raised them again.

Four Signs You Need to Increase Your Prices

Even if the thought of increasing your prices makes you feel a little sick, there are some undeniable signs that will help you determine whether it's time. Ask yourself:

1. Are you booked out, overcapacity, or have a long waiting list?

2. Do you attract 'I-need-it-now' clients who ask for fast turnarounds, but don't charge enough to make that worthwhile?

3. Do you have high-maintenance clients who are no longer worth working with at your current prices?

4. Are your results incredible, and do clients often say you've changed their lives?

If you answered 'yes' to three or more of these questions, it's time to increase your prices! Nobody is going to give you permission' you have to claim it for yourself, and decide that you're worth it and that *now* is the perfect time. Let's dig into these signs a little deeper.

Sign #1: You're Booked Out

Are you in such demand that you're booked out for weeks, if not months, in advance? Time for a price increase. Are you seeing clients back to back with no time in between to grab a cup of tea or take a quick pee? I've been there! Remember, I used to get up at 5 a.m. for my first international client of the day and had all-day sessions without a break.

Sound familiar? One biz friend told me that she once peed in a towel during a call because she had no time for a toilet break! This is not good, but highly relatable. I didn't do the towel thing, but I'd mute myself on the phone so I could sneak to the bathroom and relieve myself without my client overhearing.

It's nice to be popular, but if your client schedule is starting to impact your life (or your bladder), it's a sign you're ready to increase your prices. In fact, you can increase your rates and the demand probably won't drop off that much. *Trust me on this.* A long waiting list is a big sign that you're too inexpensive for your reputation or for the results that you give people. Before you try and justify this, let me first say that everyone's version of 'booked out' is different. Your capacity is entirely personal.

Pricing is all about supply and demand. If you have a lot of people clamoring for your services, chances are that you can afford to increase your prices, at least a little bit – if not a lot. Working an over-demanding schedule because you can't say no is unsustainable, and one of the ways you can recalibrate demand is to charge more in alignment with your actual value in the marketplace. No more metaphorical (or literal) peeing in towels!

The bonus is that you'll work less and either earn the same amount or *more* money than before. And you'll have more energy to serve your clients or to reclaim some creative space to focus on other projects, like writing a book or creating a course, that could help you serve even more people.

Now, you might resist this because it feels like cheating if you're earning more for doing less. If that's the case, it's time to reread Part I: Mindset to work on your blocks and Part II: Business Models to find a model that causes less stress.

— *Lesson* —

**Being booked out is often a sign that
you're charging too little.**

Sign #2: You're Attracting 'I-Need-It-Now' Clients

'Fast, Cheap, and Good... you can only pick two.'

ANON

You can't be extremely good at what you do, deliver results faster than everyone else, *and* be the cheapest in the market. That's a recipe for disaster, and not even remotely chill. You might have a reputation for being the 'emergency go-to girl' who does things quickly, or maybe you're just a sucker for sob stories. It's flattering to be in demand, but it's more fun to make money and not live in stress all the time, especially if you've developed a reputation for being someone who can fix disasters.

I've heard lots of horror stories. For example, the résumé writer who worked all weekend to finish a client's 'emergency' request (without asking for payment up front), and the client then ghosted after receiving the CV. Unfortunately, this is way too common. Some clients urgently need a logo by the end of the week, even though they've failed for months to provide the necessary design information. Some coaching clients 'desperately' need to talk *today* due to their own bad time management (I'll admit I've been *that* client, but I'm always prepared to pay for it!)

Do you need lots of time and space to do your work, or do you love the adrenaline rush of finishing jobs quickly and meeting intense deadlines? Your capacity is a huge consideration when setting and increasing prices, as is your lifestyle. Do you really want to work evenings and weekends for little money and ungrateful clients? Hell, no!

The problem is that many women unwittingly create this scenario by saying yes to last-minute requests and not charging enough in the first place. If you keep attracting clients who are disorganized and expect you to fix their problems, you either need to change your marketing, put some new boundaries in place, or create a whole new offering with a price that works for you. Recognizing the fact that you're attracting high-maintenance clients is actually an opportunity to create a lucrative premium service for your business.

You could set two-tiered pricing: a standard one and another to 'jump the queue,' for impatient people like me. For example, if your wait time is now several weeks or months, you could easily increase your prices. But if you added a premium service, you could cut the wait-time down to a week. Here's how that works: you could allocate three days a week to regular clients who have to wait in a queue. But you could reserve one or two days a week for people who don't mind paying a premium to see you sooner.

Does that feel unfair? Why? Lots of businesses offer this kind of service, and people don't balk at paying more for certain things. You pay extra to online retailers to have your package delivered faster, right? Why shouldn't you do it too?

Some businesses use the higher premiums paid by 'express service' customers to keep prices low in other areas. So, if you feel bad about charging for fast-track service, you could use a portion of the proceeds to create scholarships for people who couldn't otherwise afford you. And by the way, just because what you do is easy and fun for you, doesn't mean it should be cheap for clients. Fast turnarounds are a premium service no matter how long it takes you to complete a project.

> *'Poor planning on your part does not*
> *necessitate an emergency on mine.'*
> BOB CARTER

Tips for Offering Premium/Fast-Track Services

✦ **Plan ahead.** If you work in an industry in which rush jobs are the norm, *create space in your schedule in advance* to accommodate inevitable last-minute requests.

✦ **Get organized now with crystal-clear contracts, terms, and conditions.** Rushed verbal agreements can go haywire, and you're more likely to make (and regret) them when you're under pressure.

✦ **Know and communicate the process.** Specify precisely what is and isn't included in each of your services, exactly what you need from the client, and *when* you need it. That way, you set clear expectations up front and minimize the chance of scope creep.

✦ **Automate the process.** If you need clients to fill in a form before you start work, make this an automated email with automated follow-ups. Use an online scheduler so you're not wasting time with endless emails. Consider outsourcing or batching some of the work too.

✦ **Get paid up front** (or at least take a hefty deposit). Don't release or ship the final product until you receive payment in full. Urgency gives you more power in this situation, so now's your time to be clear about your boundaries.

Charging for Fast-Track Work

Some service-based entrepreneurs add a certain percentage (anything from 10 to 50 percent) to their standard rate for rush work. Others have one price for their usual timeframe and another for a faster turnaround. Charging a premium rate can feel scary, but as I said, it's standard in almost every industry. The key is to identify a cost that gives clients what they need *and* feels good for you.

Lastly, reframe a 'rush job' into premium service. It's all about marketing. *Don't make your clients wrong for wanting quick results!*

Instead of berating them for being disorganized or framing your premium price as a penalty fee, make it something positive. Call it a 'VIP rate' or a chance for them to 'skip the queue,' so they'll feel special instead of penalized.

Whatever you decide, attracting these clients is a tremendous opportunity to serve people who want instant gratification – or who have more money than time (like me). Just make sure you charge accordingly!

— *Lesson* —

Instant gratification should cost more.

Sign #3:
You're Attracting High-Maintenance Clients

One of my Money Bootcampers, creative coach Bonnie Gillespie, told me that her motto used to be 'drama costs more,' but after working on her money blocks, she now says, 'drama is someone else's client.' Ah, that feels so much better!

Most entrepreneurs have a low point in their business when they think, *This isn't worth it. I should just get a job.* You've been there, right? If you're attracting clients who always complain, try to negotiate on price, nitpick your work, and generally make your life hell, it's a *huge* sign that you're an energetic mismatch to your current pricing.

It's the universe's way of forcing your hand to increase your prices, not a sign that you should quit your business, that you're in the wrong line of work, or you're not 'cut out' for being in business. Please listen, otherwise those nightmare clients will keep coming! You deserve to have clients who gladly pay you for what you do without stress or drama.

When you charge too little, you think, *I'm delivering so much, and I'm trying to make it so affordable. Why aren't they happy and grateful?* It's not the price. You're an energetic match to people who don't appreciate you because you're not appreciating *yourself*. You're just attracting clients who mirror the energy you're projecting.

Many women ignore the signs and work with someone because they feel obligated to – not because they feel like a fit. Listen to your gut. Pay attention to the red flags that tell you someone has the potential to be a painful client. You can recognize these people by their demands for a discount when you know you're already affordable, requests for accommodations above and beyond what you're comfortable with, and the constant overstepping of boundaries.

Do you feel good or resentful when you work with a client? When you charge appropriately for what you do, you'll attract those who mirror your self-worth back to you. Plus, when you're not desperate for every single client, you'll feel empowered to say no to the ones you know aren't going to work out!

My friend Natalie MacNeil, an author and coach, calls this a 'fuck off price.' She says, 'This is your internal, pre-determined number of what you're willing to work for. If the client isn't willing to pay *at least* this as a minimum, then you can absolutely say no to the project, no questions asked.'

Natalie says her fuck off price came from the 80/20 rule: the lowest-paying 20 percent of her clients were the ones who caused the greatest amount of stress. Increasing her prices helped her focus on clients who actually appreciated her. You don't have to work with painful people. Increase your prices and often, they go away!

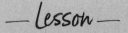

— *Lesson* —

High-maintenance clients are never worth the money!

Sign #4: Your Results Are Incredible

Someone recently told me that she wanted to lower the price of her coaching packages because she was so good at getting results that her clients ran out of things to talk about in multiple sessions. She basically 'cured' them in one session, so she wanted to reduce her prices drastically because she felt guilty. Hell, no!

I don't know about you, but I'd pay a premium to work with someone who was so good that she could get me better results in less time. I highly value speed and efficiency, and I'm willing to pay for it!

There's a price point for every market and budget, and that's true of any business. Lots of industries have tiered pricing, like consulting firms and even hair salons (senior stylists are more expensive than apprentices). Experience often means better results for your clients, and the better you get, the more you can justify higher prices. After all, you can help save or make your clients a *lot* of money when you're fantastic at what you do. That's why business is the ultimate meritocracy. If you get amazing results for your clients, you deserve to charge accordingly!

But here's the problem: many women in business vastly underestimate their value to clients. Sometimes you need to do research and quantify it for yourself. For example, advertising specialists might look at the return on investment their clients are getting for the ad money they spend. Coaches can quantify whether they've helped people to lose weight, find love, or hit other personal goals. What value would your clients put on something that's *priceless*?

Don't forget that your knowledge didn't come to you for free. Your clients are borrowing your years of education and experience so they don't have to learn on their own through trial and error. They're paying you to shortcut their success and give them the best results possible. Your investment in mastering your craft saves them time and money. Remember to factor that in to your pricing. Experience gives you the right to charge more for what you offer, especially when you create results that have an impact on your clients' time, income, happiness, love life, health, security, or desire for a better life. I'll teach you how to (ethically) tap into these desires in the Marketing section.

EXERCISE: KNOWING YOUR VALUE

After looking at all the clear signs that you should increase your prices, ask yourself the following questions:

- Is demand outstripping my available energy right now? How many clients would I like instead, and for what money?

- Do I want to offer a 'skip the queue' or fast turnaround service? If so, what would make it worthwhile?

- Do I need a 'fuck off price' to deter painful clients? If so, what would feel good?

- Am I undervaluing the results I give to clients?

And then take action! Add a new service to your website, set new prices, or set some new boundaries for clients.

— *Lesson* —

Amazing results can attract a higher price.

Announcing Your New Prices

The simple way to break the news about your new prices is to announce them – just tell people the new prices. The more complicated way is to second-guess them a million times, chicken out of telling anyone, backtrack a few times, vacillate between the old and the new prices, and then finally bite the bullet and feel like vomiting every time you say your prices. Ask me how I know this.

The method for picking a new price is the same as for setting the original one: *you just pick a number.* I've muscle-tested numbers, I've used random number generator websites, and I've literally flipped a coin. You could add 10 percent (or any percentage) to your current packages or pick a number that's visually pleasing or meaningful to you.

Stop thinking there's a special pricing strategy; most people are winging it (and second-guessing it) as much as you are! You'll realize pretty quickly if there's a mismatch and you can tweak it accordingly. There are no rules about how often you can change your prices – there's no pricing police!

The most important thing to deal with is the fear. You'll convince yourself that nobody will ever pay your new rate and that taking this step will spark a downward spiral into bankruptcy and homelessness. Then (trust me), one day, someone will pay the new price, and you'll feel relieved for a while – until it's time to increase it, and the cycle starts all over!

It's normal to feel nervous, so always remind yourself that it's *okay* to make money doing what you love. You're allowed to be successful, charge more than others in your industry, and have a wildly profitable business. You have to believe in the value you're creating for your customers and then be unattached to the outcome. Remember, some people will complain, some will think it's a steal. No big deal. To be really chill about this, you need a plan, so I've got some specific advice for:

❖ Increasing prices for existing clients

❖ Transitioning a freebie into a paid client

❖ Increasing prices for a course, program, or for new clients

Increasing Prices for Existing Clients

Some of your clients are getting an absolute bargain, and it's high time to increase your prices. How does that sentence make you feel? Terrified or relieved? It's natural if you're scared about losing some clients. And I'll be honest: some people won't want to continue working with you at your new price. But that's okay. Some customers happily shop at both Target and Armani, but that's not usually the case. You can't force a Target customer to pay Armani prices, and vice versa.

Most women feel that charging more excludes people, but the truth is that you *can't* serve everyone. As you charge more for your work, you won't be able to take all your customers with you – especially the ones you served during your entrepreneurial apprenticeship (your Target days).

We often think that, if we price ourselves out of someone's budget, nobody else will help them. But this 'savior' syndrome can burn you out, make you feel resentful and cynical about your business, and limit the impact you can truly make in the world because you have no extra energy to give.

If some of your customers are no longer aligned with your pricing, it creates space for someone else to serve them at rates they can afford. It creates opportunities for new people in your industry to learn their craft and become leaders in their field. You're no longer an apprentice and, since you're your own boss, *you* have to promote yourself and give yourself a higher salary.

Maybe your expertise has increased rapidly since you first started out. Or you've invested a ton in your business and personal growth, so you're adding even more value to your clients. Or, now that you've been working on your money blocks, you simply know that you're worth more. You might even realize that these clients are costing you money or other opportunities. This is especially true if you find yourself feeling resentful or that the energy exchange between you is unequal.

Guess what? You're not trapped. You're allowed to charge more, no matter how long you've been working together. You didn't sign up for a lifetime of servitude.

Below is a 'script' for communicating a new price to an existing client. This works best for clients who are coming to the end of an agreed timeframe or project, but you can adapt it for those open-ended clients too. You can do this over the phone (which is best) or via email (which is still okay). Either way, you can read it out word-for-word so you don't get nervous. (You can download all the scripts in this section at Chillpreneur.com/Bonus. You can customize them to suit your particular circumstances.)

Before you talk to your client, read my guidelines for successful money conversations below.

Tips for Price Increase Conversations

✤ **Remind yourself of the immense value you add to your client's life.** Take a moment to affirm to yourself: 'I'm worth every cent!' You might reread testimonials the client has sent you or review the outcome of the work you've done together.

✤ **Have the conversation at the start of your session or meeting, not the end.** That way, you won't chicken out or end it with any awkward money talk.

✤ **Pause and breathe** in between each sentence, to let them add their thoughts or agree with you. It stops you from speaking too quickly, or sounding nervous and, if they love working with you, let them tell you and sell themselves!

✤ **Keep it light and don't ask permission.** This is not a negotiation process – it's a heads-up, so you don't need to apologize or justify your decision.

✤ **Don't feel rushed.** If they have questions, take a note and say you'll answer them after their session is over. Clients shouldn't have to pay for the time in which you're explaining your new prices, so make sure you add extra time to their session at the end.

Script for Existing Clients

Before we get started today, I just want to remind you that your current package with me ends on [date].

[Pause for a moment and let the client speak.]

I'm really proud of the work we've done together, including...

[List some of the things they've achieved as a result of your work together, particularly as it relates to increased revenue or success for them. Pause for a moment and let them respond.]

I'd love to continue working with you to take your [business/ life/health] to the next level. You're such a great client to work with!

[Pause to let them respond.]

I'm discontinuing this current package, but I'd love to transition you into my new [awesome package name], which I think is much more appropriate for where you're going in your life/ business.

[Briefly explain the new benefits. It genuinely has to feel as if you're graduating them to the next level, not just charging more for the same thing.]

Because you're one of my existing clients, I'll also give you [a VIP day, free access to another program, or some other benefit] as a thank-you for renewing your contract.

The investment for the new program is $x, and I have a payment plan available. I'll send you an email that contains all the information you need to renew.

You don't have to decide today – this is just a heads-up before the current package ends. Do you have any initial questions?

[Definitely stop talking here.]

Okay, I'll send you an email about the new package soon. Now, let's get started with today's agenda. Are you okay if we go an extra [amount] minutes to make up for the time we spent on this?

Note that I recommend offering a bonus when you increase your prices, as a way of rewarding repeat customers. Remember the warning I gave earlier: don't be too generous and over-deliver in an attempt to 'bribe' your clients. The result they get by working with you *is* the reward. The bonus is just a cherry on top! The bonus you offer can be extra time with you (not too much), access to another course or program you offer, or some additional things that don't cost you too much time or energy (which just perpetuates the problem).

To come up with the most appropriate bonuses, I create a matrix with perceived value on one axis and my investment (in time, energy, and money) on the other. I brainstorm everything I'd like to offer in a package and plot it all out. Then I pick one or two bonuses that make the most sense. You'll find the template for a blank matrix among the book bonuses at Chillpreneur.com/Bonus. Think win-win. Don't give away the farm, as that will defeat the purpose of a price increase!

After the session, you can follow up via email with the details of your new package (have this pre-written), and during the next few meetings, remind your client of the deadline for both your rebooking incentive and your price increase. Every single time, follow up with an email that contains the information they need to sign up. Some people want to take action right away. Make it easy for them to give you money.

In your last meeting with your client, *ask for the sale*. It's totally okay if they say no, but if you don't ask, you'll never know!

Transitioning a Freebie into a Paying Client

People you haven't charged before might be ones you've been bartering with, have been working with in exchange for a testimonial, or just feel bad about charging. Either way, get clear about the value you offer and the value of a client having invested in themselves. Receiving something for free versus paying for it results in a totally different energy and accountability. Give clients the gift of investing in themselves!

The script for this is pretty much the same as the one above, with a few variations.

Script for a Freebie Client

Before we get started, I just want to remind you that your free sessions with me end on [date].

I'm really proud of the work we've done together, including...

[List some of the things they've achieved as a result of your work together, particularly as it relates to increased revenue or success for them.]

I'd love to continue working with you to take your [business/life/health] to the next level. We seem to be a great fit.

When our free sessions end, I'd like to transition you into my [awesome package name], which I think is a great next step for where you're going in your [life/business/health].

As a special bonus for coming on board as an official client, I'll also give you [a VIP day, free access to another program, or some other benefit] to reward you for committing to your success.

The investment for the program is [amount], and I have a payment plan available. I'll send you an email containing a link to all the details you need to sign up.

You don't have to decide today, but do you have any initial questions?

[Stop talking here.]

Okay, I'll send you an email soon. Now, let's get started with today's session.

Increasing Prices for a Course or New Client

In theory, this is the easiest one. Just stick your new rates on your website and new clients or students will pay the new prices. But as we've discussed so many times in this book, easy on the outside means nothing when it comes to money. Raising your prices for people who haven't worked with you before is actually a really great sales opportunity. I've used this as a brilliant strategy: both with one-on-one coaching services and courses.

It's totally fine to increase the price as your results, quality, and value increase. My Money Bootcamp has had five different price points as I've added more value to the course! Each increase provided an opportunity for a 'Get it now!' marketing campaign, so don't increase a price without a big announcement that gives people one last chance at the old price.

If you're a service-based business, send personalized messages to anyone who has expressed interest in your services in the past year. It might be the perfect time, and they'll be bummed out if they've been quietly saving up to work with you and didn't know about your price increase. Send them a simple message like this:

Script for a New Client

I'm touching base about working together this year. I have a few spots available on my calendar and want to let you know that my prices are going up on [date].

I'd love to help you achieve your goals, and I think we'd be a great fit because [explain why].

If you decide to sign up before [date] you'll get the current price of [amount] and, as a special bonus, I'll also give you [a VIP day, free access to another program, or some other benefit] to reward you for committing to your success.

The current investment for the program is [amount], and I have a payment plan available.

You'll find all the details and booking information for my current prices here: [link]. After [date], the new price will be [amount].

Would you like to have a brief conversation about working together? You can book a time to talk on my calendar here: [link]

Honestly, you don't have to overcomplicate it. Just be really clear that your prices are going up and they have to take some action to work with you at your old rates.

More Tips for Increasing Prices

✦ **Give people notice** of exactly when your prices are going up – 15–30 days in advance is the perfect time, or at the end of the month.

✦ **Reach out to people** who have been 'thinking' about working with you and give them an excuse to get off the fence before your rates increase.

✦ **Give regular reminders**, both in your newsletter and social media, to encourage people to get in at the current rates, before they go up!

✦ **Create urgency!** Put a countdown timer on your sales page.

✦ **Show integrity** – actually change the prices on your website and marketing materials after the deadline. Don't chicken out. This small but symbolic action will make you feel like it's real!

Resisting Increasing Your Prices?

Let's talk about a mindset shift you need to make before increasing your rates. You might be saying, 'Nobody will ever pay this new price,' and if you believe that, you actually might struggle at first.

I noticed this in myself when I offered an 'early bird discount' for my Money Bootcamp. I told myself, *Nobody will pay full price for this*. And guess what – nobody did! Well, hardly anyone. Ninety-five percent of people took the early bird offer. At the next launch, I told myself: *This is amazing value, even at full price*, and that time, just 70 percent of registrations were early bird. Nothing had changed except my belief that it was still worth it at the higher price. You might need to go back and read client testimonials to remind yourself of the same thing.

You don't have to make huge price jumps. You might need to acclimatize to new price points every few months. There are no rules, it doesn't have to be annual, and you can do it whenever you like!

EXERCISE: GETTING READY FOR A PRICE INCREASE

In your journal or in a conversation with an entrepreneurial friend, answer the following questions:

- Are you okay with letting some of your customers go?

- What limiting belief is behind your reluctance to charge more?

- What would you like your new prices to be?

- On what date are your prices going up?

Then take action based on your answers!

— *Lesson* —

You're the boss! Give yourself a pay increase.

You might really resist the idea of raising your prices and procrastinate about acting on this chapter. Just remember that you're in business to make money, and you're allowed to profit from your skills and talents.

Money is power. The more collective wealth we have as women, the more independence and control we have over our own lives. When you make more, you pay more taxes into the system to support others and reduce your own burden on public services. You can support political candidates who can enact change on a large scale, and you can put your money behind creating a better and more just world for everyone.

The world will become a much better place when more women prosper financially and are financially independent, including *you*! Charging what you're worth is the first step.

— CHAPTER 10 —

Awkward Money Conversations Made Easy

*M*y biz friends and I laugh about the fact that being in business is just a series of potentially awkward and scary money conversations. Unfortunately, these very normal situations are just too much for some entrepreneurs. But don't let any of them stop you from playing the game of business. Back to the snakes (chutes) and ladders analogy: this *is* the game!

Just like having people unsubscribe from your newsletter, having to talk to people about money is an inevitable and *unavoidable* rite of passage. Don't be surprised when weird stuff happens. The truth is that people will make unreasonable requests all the time! Clients will be demanding and ask for exceptions to your policies. They'll ask for discounts or freebies. Some will demand refunds and others will default on their commitments to you.

But it's honestly no big deal and is just part of being in business. The rewards are worth a few awkward moments, and they're why you need some business besties. Together, you can call or text each other, say 'WTF!' and laugh at the audacity of some people. Women often struggle with these money conversations because we believe we have 'no choice': we want to be accommodating and 'nice,' and we want people to like us. But nothing drains your energy faster than saying yes when you really want to shout *no!*

You don't have to make exceptions, you don't have to help everyone, and you don't have to feel bad about it (even though the first few times you say no you'll feel like a mean ole bitch!) It will make you feel better to know that it happens to everyone. I've experienced every single one of these scenarios multiple times, and I can tell you that it gets easier. The requests don't stop; you'll just get 'gatekeepers' who'll stop you having to deal with it yourself, or you'll just feel less bad about saying no.

Strategies for Awkward Money Talks

Remember, what scares you today, won't scare you tomorrow! I'm not a big fan of confrontation, but I've some really simple strategies for handling the difficult money conversations that *I guarantee* you'll have to deal with too.

- ❖ **Get a gatekeeper.** You don't have to be the one to hold all of these conversations. Your assistant (or fake assistant) can help you with this – everyone needs a 'Dave from accounts.' (I'll explain who he is later.)

- ❖ **Boundaries are your friend**. You don't have to put up with rude behavior or unreasonable requests just because there's money involved.

- ❖ **Assume that people want to pay you.** You'll feel a lot more empowered doing that than you will second-guessing whether you're worth paying in the first place.

✦ **Where possible, follow a script** (examples coming up). That way, you won't chicken out or say the wrong thing. It's so much easier, especially when you're on the phone.

✦ **Practice clarity.** Before you send anything by email, take out all the apologetic or unclear language you've used to try and be the 'nice girl' or avoid hurting feelings.

✦ **Create a bank of 'canned responses.'** You or your assistant can customize and send these without thinking too much about them (you'll find some examples in this chapter and in the book bonuses at Chillpreneur.com/Bonus).

✦ **Update your policies.** People seem to respect things that are in black and white, so if something is a recurring problem for you, make it an official policy on your website's terms and conditions and/or in your contracts.

> *'Balance is not better time management, but better boundary management. Balance means making choices and enjoying those choices.'*
>
> BETSY JACOBSON

'Can I Pick Your Brain?'

When you're starting out, it's flattering to have people ask you for advice. Requests can range from a subtle, 'Hey, what do you think of this?' to a blatant, 'Can you help me?' These requests will come from friends, family, peers, competitors, and even random strangers. You'll be shocked how entitled people can get when you start to make a name for yourself. This is where women with 'go-to girl' personalities can get stuck because we want to be helpful and solve problems. Any problems.

I used to be everyone's agony aunt, travel agent, business coach, and general mini-Oprah. That started in school and continued into my working life. I just couldn't say no to requests for help, and I couldn't resist solving particularly tricky dilemmas, even if they weren't my business specialty!

If you're a go-to entrepreneur, this can quickly result in you giving away your genius for nothing. It's pretty rare that back-and-forth emails giving free advice turn into paid work. In fact, it comes at a huge cost to you. Most of the time, you actually can't solve people's problems over email – at least not in a sustainable way. People need to invest in themselves and solve the problem with an expert – you. So, you're doing them a disservice by enabling them to keep procrastinating or by putting a temporary bandage on the issue.

The tricky thing about social media now is that there are so many ways for people to contact you: it's an introvert's nightmare! These 'brain picks' might come in the comments on a social media post, a sneaky private message, or via email, and they can quickly get overwhelming. If a member of one of my paid programs wants extra information on a lesson, I generally say something like this:

Script #1 for a Brain-Picker

Great to hear from you – and great question!

I can't answer private questions about this course, but if you ask it publicly in our networking group and tag me, everyone can benefit from my answer, and you'll get input from other members, too.

If the brain-picker isn't in a paid program, I say I'll answer the question in an upcoming blog post or, if it's something that can be solved in one of my paid programs, I point them there. **You. Don't. Owe. People. Free. Information.** Your time is valuable, but others will value it only if you do first. A straightforward way to deal with brain-pickers is to:

✦ Acknowledge their question.

✦ Express sympathy.

✦ Tell them you have a solution.

✦ Tell them how to get that solution from you.

For example:

Script #2 for a Brain-Picker

Thanks so much for your message. It sounds like you're in a really challenging situation.

My program is perfectly designed for people in your circumstances and can help you in the following ways [list of benefits].

You'll find all the details here: [link].

Your reply doesn't have to be long or apologetic, because the logical next step for brain-pickers is to work with you! Assume that's what they want in the first place. If you're getting into long back-and-forths with people asking random questions, then you can create a FAQ on your website and point them to that.

What about people who want to meet for 'coffee,' but you know that actually means 'free advice?' I prefer to assume they want to be a client, so I send a similar message to the one above.

Script #3 for a Brain-Picker

Great to hear from you, and thanks for your interest in my business.

My schedule can't accommodate a meet-up, but I'd love to help you out. It sounds like my mentoring package might be the best option for you.

You'll find details and scheduling here: [link].

If they write back and say, 'Oh no, I just want to meet you for a casual coffee!' or want free advice, you can elaborate and say something like:

Script #4 for a Brain-Picker

Thanks for your interest in meeting with me. Unfortunately, I can't meet because the time I don't spend with clients is dedicated to my family.

But seriously, if you love meeting with people, *do it.* It can be a great way to make new friends. Just make sure you don't coach or mentor them during the meet-up. That's for your paying clients. Keep it light, and if they ask for specific business advice during the meet-up, you can say something like:

Script #5 for a Brain-Picker

It's difficult to give advice when I don't know the whole situation, and I'm not your official coach. How about I send you information about my rates and packages when I'm back in the office?

Setting Boundaries

It's also okay to protect your time (and your Golden Goose) by saying no. Have you noticed that the people who demand the most free help are also the least gracious? I've given advice to people via email or coffee dates and never received an expression of gratitude in return, and often, I had to pay for my own coffee anyway!

Setting boundaries around offering free advice needs to become a *practice*. The first time you do it, you'll probably feel mean, but put yourself in their shoes and consider what's in their highest good. If you have an excellent solution for them, don't get sucked into giving them a sub-par experience via email or in-person advice without accountability. Hold them to a better standard so they get better results.

I *still* have to be disciplined about not responding to brain-pickers' requests. One came through as I was writing this chapter and I had to restrain myself from stopping work and sending them free advice. The truth is: people who want to take advantage of you will never go away. The only thing you can do to prevent yourself from dispensing free advice is to establish better boundaries and redirect brain-pickers to the paid service you offer.

Lastly, see if there's a reason you're attracting brain-pickers. Are you afraid to charge? Are you training people to get your valuable services for free by always being available and never saying no? You're worth the money you're charging!

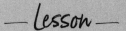

— *Lesson* —

Giving people advice for free isn't in their best interest.

'Can I Have A Discount?'

I was shopping recently and noticed something interesting: some brands never go on sale and don't give discounts.

I found a tiny rack in fashion outlet Country Road marked 'Last of the bestsellers' with a discreet discount sticker on each item. The message was 'This isn't our crappy stuff, we're almost out of our most popular stock, and this is your last chance to buy it.' Then I noticed that on workout clothing brand lululemon's website, there isn't a 'sale' tab: instead, there's a section called 'We made too much.' They don't want to be perceived as a discount retailer – especially in their flagship stores – and they don't want to train their customers to expect regular discounts or to wait until things go on sale.

Maybe you think this is just semantics; however, there's an *energy* behind the way you frame discounts. Are you known for always offering a discount or are people happy to pay your full prices? It's totally okay to say 'I don't offer discounts or scholarships' without having to justify anything! I'm not saying you should never offer financial incentives for your customers, but the way you market them and the reason behind them are really important.

Here are some script ideas for you:

Script for an 'Early Bird' Incentive

I don't offer a discount, but if you purchase by [date], you can take advantage of my early bird offer.

I love rewarding action-takers, so I often give a financial incentive to people who buy on the first day, either by offering an actual discount (that's okay in this case) or by offering a bonus. Here's the thing: you have to be strict on this. If you don't stick to your date or quantity policy, you're sending the message that what you do isn't worth full price, and you're training people that deadlines don't matter.

Script for a 'Package' incentive

I don't offer a discount, but if you purchase my [awesome name] package, you can get six sessions for the price of four.

Packages are always my preferred recommendation, especially for service-based companies, because it's way less work for you and better accountability for your clients. Even though my initial private coaching rate was low, I created packages of six because that gave the best results for my clients. Eventually, I took on only clients who would commit to six months or more. Packages are good for your clients. If you're realistic and honest about what clients need to achieve excellent results, one session with you just isn't going to cut it, right?

Script for a 'Returning Client' Incentive

I don't normally offer a discount, but because you're a returning client, I'd be happy to book you at the old rate [or offer an additional bonus]. This offer expires on [date].

When you've worked with people before (and only if you liked working with them), you might want to offer a limited-time incentive or added value if they rebook with you. If your prices have increased since they originally booked, your incentive could be that they continue at their old rate – but only if they rebook within a specific timeframe. Bonuses are good too – just follow the win-win rule.

Script for a 'Pay-In-Full' Incentive

I'd love to offer you the special rate of [amount] if you book by [date] and pay in full.

I don't mind offering payment plans, but I also love incentivizing people who want to pay in full by offering a slight discount (and some people *love* that), especially around tax time when they're trying to maximize their business deductibles.

Script for the 'Buy Everything' Incentive

I don't offer a discount on that service, but if you buy this package, you'll save [amount] overall.

I've bundled some of my bestselling courses and offered a significant discount on the set. Some people just want all your stuff in one go, so give it to them! As before, boundaries are essential: be firm in your expectations of what people need to do to be eligible for special offers and incentives.

Introductory/Beta Pricing

What about your first-ever course or program? Many women think they should offer a trial run or introductory price if they're new or starting out. You might have heard this called a 'beta price.'

I'm firmly against this. Why? Because the energy is all wrong. When you offer a beta price, the power dynamic is off. Your participants go into 'review mode' and aren't fully experiencing the true transformation of being a paying client. They feel like they're doing *you* a favor and can often be way more critical because they're experiencing your program as a reviewer not a student. You've given them an energetic 'out' from doing the actual work.

You can, however, offer a 'special introductory price,' which is basically the same thing but energetically different. It feels celebratory, as if people are lucky to be the first participants. Be clear that future customers will have to pay a higher price and stick to it!

— *Lesson* —

Reframe discounts into incentives!

What about Pay-What-You-Want Promotions?

I get asked this a lot, and you might not like my answer. I don't love pay-what-you-want (PWYW) for services because most of the time, you're just chickening out of actually setting a price. You might think you're being generous and flexible, but often your customers spend a lot of time worrying if they are under- or overpaying.

Some people use PWYW as a way to gain approval or test their value to others, and then feel rejected and unvalued by what people choose to pay. With PWYW pricing, you'll still need to get the offer out to lots of people and, if they don't take you up on it, that, too, can feel like rejection.

As a customer, I *never* buy things on PWYW because it forces me to do the pricing work that others failed to do. That stresses me out: *just tell me the price and I'll pay it!*

Tips for Offering Pay-What-You-Want

If you still feel drawn to it, here are a few guidelines:

✦ **Be genuinely unattached to the outcome.** Don't obsess over the individual amounts people pay. Look at the overall result, not who paid what.

✦ **Set boundaries.** Limit the timeframe and number of people who can take up the offer. Make this a special event and emphasize that it's a one-time thing.

✦ **Give a realistic price guideline.** For example, display clearly what the service would usually cost, or give a realistic scale so people don't worry about over- or underpaying. Remember, a confused mind always says no.

✦ **Be clear in your ask.** If there's an expectation – for example, that people have to give you a testimonial in return for their offer – say so in advance and follow up.

- ❖ **Value your time**. Don't offer PWYW for one-on-one time; it works much better with e-products or courses. Otherwise, you'll have to cap how many you can realistically deliver.

- ❖ **Set your limits**. If there's a price you wouldn't accept, be upfront about it and set that boundary (if possible, by using software that enables you to set a minimum). Otherwise, people *will* take advantage of you.

Again, be genuinely unattached – you'll get people who hardly pay anything and others who overpay. I've heard of people paying literally one cent, so go into this with your eyes wide open.

— *Lesson* —

Make sure you're not using PWYW because you're chickening out of setting prices.

'Can We Barter?'

I wrote about this in *Get Rich, Lucky Bitch*, but want to reemphasize it: I'm firmly in the 'no bartering' camp. Why? Simply put, bartering has a detrimental impact on your ability to earn money, and it's a trap that too many women fall into.

Bartering means swapping your products and services for somebody else's without money ever changing hands. It seems like an excellent idea for women – especially at the start of your business, when you have little money. What could go wrong? Plenty! Have you fulfilled your end of the bargain and received something crappy in return? Or did the person you bartered with fail to fulfill the swap *at all*, leaving you feeling taken advantage of? It rarely works. Sometimes, you agree to a bartering arrangement out of obligation or guilt, even if you don't need the service the other person is exchanging.

It sets up a weird power dynamic, which is particularly true if you're both coaches and coach each other for free. Being both the expert and the client is *hard* and not particularly useful for either of you. If there's someone you'd love to collaborate with, set up an informal mastermind or accountability group, rather than swapping your services. Respect each other.

Declare Yourself Open to Paying Clients

The biggest reason I discourage bartering is the symbolism of it. I understand that bartering feels convenient, collaborative, and even 'post-money.' It feels warm, fuzzy, and generous to help each other without 'dirty money' polluting your relationship. But we live in a society in which women are already financially disadvantaged. Why continue to perpetuate an environment in which we don't have actual, spendable money?

If you aspire to have a thriving business (and quit your day job), then bartering can stop the flow of money into your business. You're not open for business literally or energetically. Bartering sends out a message that you're willing to work for free, and that can cause you to attract clients who don't respect your prices. It's a highly symbolic milestone to receive money for what you do and to pay others in return. Trading money is much cleaner than bartering, even if it means you have to do bookkeeping and pay taxes.

You might think it's more convenient to avoid those things by not 'complicating' transactions with payment, but that's rarely true. Plus, do you see how you're telling the universe that you're not willing to create a 'real' business because you're afraid of bookkeeping or paying taxes?

Even with the best intentions, bartering can get messy. For example, I once let one of my affiliates use her accrued commission toward coaching with me. That got complicated at tax time when she thought I owed her more money, forgetting that we had this partial payment arrangement. She should have paid me, and I should have paid her, so we had a proper record. We should have respected the transaction, even if it felt 'easier' to trade. Does that feel like an extra step? Maybe, but it can avoid practical problems later on.

If something is worth paying for, just pay for it. Respect the flow of money and each other's talents, even if it means paying taxes on the income. After all, you're in business to make money. Taxes are just an inevitable part of that and very symbolic for women.

Unexpected Benefits of a 'No Bartering' Policy

When you draw a line in the sand and refuse to swap your services, exciting things start to happen. But first, you have to energetically close down free work and declare yourself open for business. Make that decision now. Even if it feels silly to, say this out loud: *'I am no longer available physically and energetically for bartering arrangements. I declare myself open for business.'*

You have to be resolute on this. *No more.* Not even one more time. Guess what will happen? I'm not psychic, but I've seen it hundreds of times. As soon as you make this decision, you'll be tested on it. You'll get a request for bartering within the next 24 hours, and a really good offer might even tempt you. *This is just a test.*

Saying no is a symbolic rite of passage for you in your business and will open up many avenues for you to receive *actual* money. Think of it as the final test of your apprenticeship. Are you ready to pass the test and graduate to being paid for your skills and talents?

How do you turn down a bartering request (especially a well-meaning or tempting one), and not feel like a bitch? You can say something like this:

Script for Declining a Bartering Request

It's great to hear from you, and I appreciate your offer. I have a no-bartering policy because I'm focused on growing my business with paying clients. But I'll be sure to check out your services!

Clients won't suddenly rain in because you've passed this test, but you'll feel an energetic shift because you're really in business now. Barter offers usually come because people see the value in what you do. That's the good news. The bad news is that, if you say yes, you're not respecting your own value. When you put a price on your time and energy, you're energetically aligned with paying clients. You're symbolically open for business.

If you keep saying no, people will stop asking and, eventually, nobody will ask again. It's been years since anybody asked me to make a barter arrangement because I'm no longer energetically aligned to that. But it started with me saying no and declaring myself open for business.

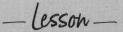

— *Lesson* —

**Saying no to bartering sends the right message –
both to potential clients and to the universe.**

'Can I Have a Friends-and-Family Discount?'

Should you offer what we call 'mates rates' in Australia to your friends and family? It depends. First of all, it's a natural thing to want to help your loved ones, and it's natural that they'll want to support your business. As usual, it only becomes a problem if it's causing you stress or keeping you from making money.

Offering discounts to friends and family can create a potentially awkward situation, but it doesn't *have* to be that way if you put a few boundaries in place. The biggest problem arises when your friends and family don't respect that your skills and talents are a commodity – especially if you're a service-based business. It doesn't appear to 'cost' you anything to do a 'quick' website for a friend or to proofread your sister's blog, but it does. It's time, energy, and expertise that you could be using for your own business, to put food on the table for your family, and to free you from your day job.

So, what should you charge them? It depends. What feels better: charging them full rates, discounted rates, or working for free? Check in with yourself and see how it feels. There's no right or wrong, but it's a useful exercise to see what objections come up in each of these scenarios.

Some of your friends will be amazing clients who will respect you, and even insist on paying your full rate. Or, if they are getting a discount, they'll be appreciative, pay you on time, and be a dream to work with. I have friends who I go to for products and services, and I have friends who've joined my courses, and it's entirely cool to pay each other's full rate. We respect each other as professionals, and there's no awkwardness.

That's the best-case scenario. I've even told some of my friends *not* to give me a discount because I just wanted to feel like a proper client who had their full attention. On the other hand, some of your loved ones should *never* be your clients, even at full rates. They might be demanding, disrespectful, and someone you'd never choose as a client, no matter how much they paid you! (I've heard the stories.)

We want our family and friends to succeed, but we aren't necessarily doing what's in their best interest by working with them. A perfect example of this is coaching loved ones. You just don't have the distance needed for that kind of relationship. They're better off working with someone who can keep them accountable, with a clean, professional relationship. Just tell them that you're too busy to help – which is true. Even if you don't have paying clients, you should be spending your time trying to find them!

— *Lesson* —

Friends and family aren't always the best clients!

If they make you feel bad (and seriously, the audacity!) remind them that this is how you earn your money, feed your family, and pay your bills. Then remind yourself that not charging them will impact your ability to make money with actual clients. Your time, energy, skills, and experience are valuable and worth paying for. Send them the name of one of your competitors, a valued peer, or even a book or course that was helpful to you. But remember, this is your business. You decide whether you work with them or not.

Script for a 'Mates Rates' Request

I'm booked out for the next six months with paid client work, so I'm not going to be able to help you this time.

Or: *I'd love to help, but I just don't have the capacity right now.*

Or: *I have a strict no friends or family policy, but I can highly recommend [name of someone else].*

If you *do* decide to go ahead, here are some guidelines:

Tips for Offering 'Mates Rates'

✤ **Decide in advance what percentage discount would feel okay** for you and would still value your time.

✤ **Treat them like a client.** Keep to your regular processes and systems, no matter what: you're allowed to keep your boundaries, even with loved ones.

✤ **Send a proper invoice with your full price shown**, even if it has a highly discounted bottom line. Show them what it would really cost to work with you.

'I Want a Refund!'

Refund requests happen. There's nothing you can do about it, and aiming for a zero refund rate is just unrealistic. Please, please, *please* don't feel bad when you get asked for a refund. It's just one of those things that happens, no matter how awesome you are, and it's something to celebrate because it means you've reached a new achievement level!

Do you want a strong and steady business? Do you want a six-figure or million-dollar business? Then refund requests are going to happen, baby! Yes, it sucks and it's unfair. It reminds you of when that kid in the playground said she didn't want to play with you. But it's *not personal*.

In fact, one rite of passage is having a client ask for a refund when you *know* they loved working with you. They were your biggest fan, then one day they went AWOL or even did a chargeback through your bank without telling you. It's heartbreaking at first, until you realize it happens to *everyone*.

Before giving you a script, I want to make sure that you have terms and conditions in place to deal with these inevitable requests. If yours haven't been revisited for a while, you may want to refresh them. Without a robust refund policy, people can just demand their money back at any time, and for the most random reasons. It's hard to deal with a refund when you have nothing in writing, which means you don't really have much power. You'll need to check for any local, state, or national laws that govern refunds, or even consult a lawyer, but whatever you do, just go sort out your policies: it's one of those annoying, but essential, things you have to do.

The first few refund requests I received were like knives in my heart. How could they not like me? It seemed unfair when they'd participated in my course and then asked for a refund at the very last moment. I've come a long way since then. The reason I can be so chill about refunds now is that:

- ❖ **I know they're inevitable**. Plus, refund rates will follow a predictable percentage over time. Watch for your own pattern, so you can budget for it.

- ❖ **It's not personal**. I've had people *rave* about my course and then ask for a refund on the last day of my money-back guarantee (because they could).

- ❖ **I have policies in place**. So I'm not making up rules on the fly or making exceptions because a client made me feel guilty.

- ❖ **My assistant deals with them**. We discuss refund requests only if the number seems unusually high (which rarely happens, but I'll talk about that in a bit).

When it comes to refunds, I highly recommend that you have a 'bad cop' on your team to deal with them. It's hard to be a supportive coach or the expert when you also have to be the Debbie Downer law enforcer. I find that people respect it more coming from someone else too, especially if they have a personal relationship with you.

Having a bad cop might sound like a cop-out (pun fully intended) but remember: being successful in business is finding your path of least resistance. If you need to have confronting conversations, you can try and get better at it, or you can act like a CEO and delegate it where possible!

My policies and my assistant are my 'bad cop,' so I don't have to be. What if you can't afford an assistant? Well, make one up! Set up another email address for your fictional assistant and answer as them. You might not feel comfortable doing this, but trust me, it will change the way you enforce boundaries in your business. My 'assistant' was called Sabrina, and she saved me again and again with her very polite but no-nonsense style, so I could take refunds less personally.

Whatever you decide, here's a script for dealing with refund requests:

Script for a Refund Request

Thank you for your message. We acknowledge your refund request.

We're ready to honor our refund policy, but before we do, is there any way we can rectify the situation? We may be able to help if we know what the problem is.

Please let us know by [date]. If we don't hear from you by then, we'll start processing your refund in accordance with our refund policy.

It's worth asking whether there's a problem that can be solved. In some cases, it's something small, like their course password won't work, or there's been a simple mistake that can be solved just by asking. Every situation like this is a chance to save the client, tighten up your refund policy, or simply follow your process and give them their money back. Making refunds easy and stress-free for people *won't* increase the amount of refund requests you get. It will, however, give people a good impression of you, and they may purchase again in the future.

I see women get defensive about refunds, want to argue back, or not give refunds out of spite. The simplest policy, in my opinion, is a no-questions-asked one, but with limits around time. Just refund it, bless them, and try not to obsess about it at 3 a.m. Be like Elsa and *let it go*.

Before we grant a refund, we ask people to fill in a very simple survey, remind them to delete copyrighted course material from any storage devices, and remove themselves from the student forum. We also ask for the reason why they requested the refund – but the honest truth is that I don't really read it. As I said earlier, feedback isn't that useful unless it's stuff you can actually fix. If you can, get someone else to read the survey, otherwise you'll probably feel really bad. If it's something like, 'Your voice is really annoying, and I didn't like it,' there's honestly not much you can do about it. But it could ruin your week. I once had someone say, 'You are teaching Satan's tools. You must be a witch!' *Allllrighty then.*

I prefer to be chill around refunds and just grant them without requiring the student to jump through too many hoops. But give refunds a specific timeline. They can't be an option forever and keep an eye on *when* people actually ask for refunds. We found most came in the first few days of the course – people often know if I'm their flavor pretty quickly – but then we noticed a lot coming right at the end, which really annoyed me.

We used to have a 60-day, 100 percent money-back guarantee but changed it after a really disheartening experience, which I *did* take personally. We had a big launch for my Money Bootcamp on October 25th one year. On December 24th, which was the last day of the money-back period, we had a record number of refund requests, including people who had enthusiastically participated in live calls, got personalized advice from me in the private networking group, and raved that the Bootcamp had changed their lives.

Merry fucking Christmas to me!

It was obvious that some people deliberately set their calendar to get the very most juice out of the course and then, during the holiday season, needed some extra cash. It felt like they stole it right out of my pocket on Christmas Eve. That was the first time I felt my generous refund policy was taken advantage of, so we changed it to 14 days, which felt right and in integrity for both myself and my clients.

I also changed the structure of the course. We held back some lessons and bonuses until after the refund period ended. Why? I had someone buy the course, download everything, create a similar Money Bootcamp, and ask for a refund on the very same day as the purchase! Yes, people can be that brazen. Don't feel bad, just live and learn!

Refund Requests After the Money-Back Period

Your answer to refund requests that come in after the refund deadline has passed can be simply 'no.' Recently, a biz friend told me she had a refund request a *year* after a customer had bought her online program. Apparently, her former student was hunting around for cash, decided to take a chance, and asked for her money back. This is way more common than you'd think. Some people are *so cheeky* and situations like that are why you need specific deadlines outlined very clearly in your refund terms.

Here's a script you can use to deal with this kind of refund:

Script for a Post-Deadline Refund Request

Thanks for your email. In regard to your refund request, our policy is a no-questions-asked money-back guarantee for [number of days] days after a program is purchased.

Because you purchased the program [number] days ago, it falls outside the refund period, and we respectfully deny your request.

Since you still have access, we recommend that you go through the program again and hope that you get value out of it.

You'll only get a few of these outrageously unreasonable requests in your career, but trust me, they will come!

Dealing with Zombie Clients

Sometimes clients purchase a package of sessions with you, or a certain amount of work, then go AWOL. They might cancel a few meetings or decide they need a break. You may suspect that their money blocks or fear got in the way. Then, a year or two later, they contact you asking to resume work, as if they hadn't ghosted you. *'I'm baaaaack! And this time I'm really ready!'* How you respond is entirely your choice. If you have solid contracts and deadlines in place, you can decline their request or get 'Sabrina' to do it.

Script for a Zombie Client

Thanks for the update on where you are with your life/health/ business.

Unfortunately, we won't be able to resume sessions under your old package because it expired on [date].

If you'd like to start a new package, I'd be delighted to work with you again. My new rates and packages are here: [link to website].

Look forward to hearing from you.

No need to get defensive or blamey. Keep it simple and direct. You can get more specific in follow-up emails if they question it. For example, you can point to the instances where they cancelled or failed to show up and prove that you sent follow-ups.

If You Have a No-Refund Policy in Place

If a refund request comes in and you didn't cover the circumstance in your policies, be honest and ask yourself:

- Did I have a clear (and written) expiration date?

- Did I provide clear instructions on how to work with me?

- Did I send reminders?

- Did I cancel sessions or otherwise hold up the process myself?

Whoever is to blame, sometimes you have to suck it up and fulfill the work, even if it's unprofitable for you. If you do, make sure you have a specific deadline in place. (Oh, and make sure it doesn't happen again by tightening up your procedures for future clients.)

It sucks to perform work at old prices when your prices have increased significantly, and it's even worse to have to provide a service that you no longer offer (or desire to offer), *especially* for people who were non-ideal clients to begin with. Here's a suggested script:

Script for a No-Refund Policy

Thanks for the update on where you are with your life/health/ business.

Normally, the package you booked expires after 12 months, but in this case, I'm willing to make an exception, as long as you book and complete all sessions by [date].

My updated terms and conditions are here [link], and here's the link for my online calendar, so you can book our final meetings [link].

After that date, my new rate will be [amount] per hour.

I look forward to working with you again.

Again, keep it simple and put the ball in their court. Send them one last reminder; tell them that your calendar is filling up quickly, and if they don't get their act together this time, their sessions will expire.

> — *Lesson* —
>
> **Your refund policy doesn't have to be**
> **complicated, but you sure do need one!**

I've put a template for my terms and conditions in the book bonuses at Chillpreneur.com/Bonus. Feel free to model your own on them. Don't use mine word-for-word though: make sure your terms and conditions are tailored to your business and reflect what's legal for your industry, state, or country.

When Your Client Defaults on a Payment

The last scenario is when (not if) clients default on a payment or decline to pay the remainder of their bill. This often happens when you offer a payment plan. In fact, we often have up to 20 percent of our monthly payment plans fail. It's a huge amount of work to recoup those costs, especially since we have hundreds of people on payment plans. This is why payment plans are more expensive. Don't feel bad about adding an additional charge to them, because payment plans *will* cost you more time, money, and potential stress.

Does that mean you shouldn't offer them? Not at all. It's still an awesome way to incentivize people who can't afford to pay the full price upfront. There's no shame in that (I've used payment plans many times to manage cash flow myself), but you have to be prepared. This is where 'Dave from accounts' comes in handy. Have you noticed that every single company in the world has a Dave in the accounts (or IT) department? When 'Dave' took over from 'Sabrina' to chase down late or default payments, we had more responses to follow-up emails. It's a gender bias that worked in our favor. Even though Dave said the same thing, for some reason, people took his requests for payment more seriously. Sad but true (test it for yourself)!

Defaults happen in every business, and it's nothing to be scared of. People's credit cards expire, they have their wallet stolen, or maybe they're short of cash one month. Don't assume that they won't or don't want to pay – they might not have even noticed. You need to follow up: in marketing or in collections, 'the fortune's in the follow-up.' Take action quickly. Send them an email right away, using very brief, non-emotive, and non-apologetic language.

Scripts for a Defaulting Client

Just letting you know that your recent payment was declined. Here's a link where you can fix that easily: [link].

Thanks for taking care of this quickly.

If you have questions or need assistance, please let us know.

(It's totally okay for you to simply ask for your money. They signed up to your product, service, or offering in good faith, and you provided it in good faith. Don't be afraid to follow up. Some people might be embarrassed and are ignoring your email. Others might not have seen it.)

Your follow-up email could be:

You might have missed the email we sent yesterday, in which we let you know that your most recent payment was declined.

Here's how you can fix that easily: [link]

If you have any questions or need help, please let us know by responding to this message as soon as you can.

Give them specific instructions. Can they click on a payment link and pay right away? Do they need to login to a system and update their card? Be accommodating but firm. If they come back asking for more time or a longer payment plan, be understanding but very clear on what you expect. Ask them to commit to a specific plan, not some vague time in the future.

Let There Be Consequences!

If things escalate, and people aren't willing to pay you, you're within your rights to tell them what the consequences will be. Again, be firm, polite, and non-emotive. Remind them of your terms and conditions of sale. Will they be removed from your program on non-payment? Does service stop? Will you withhold something until payment is made? At what point would you send them to a collections agency?

You don't have to be horrible about it. In fact, my friend Marissa Roberts, one of the nicest people in the world, uses a 'when/then' approach instead of threats:

✦ *When* you get up to date with your payments, *then* we can schedule our next session.

✦ *When* you update your credit card on file, *then* you'll get access to the course again.

✦ *When* you take care of that payment, *then* we'll make your new website live.

You can even end with 'does that sound fair enough?' Lastly, outsource this as much as possible, whether it's to 'Dave,' a real assistant, or a company that specializes in this kind of service. Play Rihanna's 'Bitch Better Have My Money' to psyche yourself up, and go get that money!

EXERCISE: GET PREPARED

1. Download the scripts from this book's bonus section and customize them, so you're ready to deal with awkward money conversations when they arise.

2. Train your team or set up your fake assistant's email address so you're ready. (Put those eighth-grade drama skills to use!)

3. Tighten up your terms and conditions so you don't have to deal with unclear policies.

~

You'll find more scripts in the book bonus section around time boundaries, how to fire suppliers, and other awkward dilemmas. None of this has to be scary; but it will happen, so be prepared! Download these resources before you forget at Chillpreneur.com/Bonus.

> — *Lesson* —
> **Charging appropriately is an act of self-care and self-love.**

— PART IV —

Marketing

Marketing

'The best marketing of all is happy clients.'
SUSAN STRIPLING

One summer, I worked for my stepdad selling second-hand fridges and washing machines. Each day, I walked around the store thinking about how much money I could make on commission and dreaming about what I'd spend it on (it was 1995, so I'm guessing it was new pointe shoes for ballet and a Tamagotchi).

But nobody ever came in. Not a *single* customer. It didn't help that it was the rainiest summer on record, or that it was a crappy store in front of my stepdad's repair shop with zero signage. So, it was just me, practicing my ballet moves on the concrete floors. I was ready to sell used white goods *like a boss*. I'd rehearsed my sales pitch. I'd prepared myself mentally for bargaining. But without customers, there's not much you can do, no matter how enthusiastic you are about the product.

I hear many entrepreneurs say they've put their heart and soul into their product, and they can't believe nobody has bought it. It's disheartening if you've overcome a lot of resistance to starting your business in the first place, only to find that it's all for nothing. Heart and soul are essential, for sure, but it's just one part of the equation.

Yes, it's important to love what you do and to love your customers. But you need people to shower your love *onto*. You need to make money to have a viable business. It doesn't matter how much love and care you put into the personalized packaging or how much emotional work went into your sales page. You need *customers*. Lighting an abundance candle isn't marketing – it's procrastination if it's your only strategy (though I do love woo-woo practices on top of actual marketing).

It's sad when nobody buys. It's sad when you've launched a new course, and there are zero sign-ups. And it's sad when you have no clients, despite being ready to change people's lives. It's easy to internalize it, and we often do. We think a lack of sales means:

* Nobody likes us.

* We're not good (or popular) enough.

* We didn't put enough heart and soul into it.

* We need a new website or a sexier logo.

I get it. It's frustrating and might trigger old memories of rejection from your school days. But now it's magnified because your rent and your ability to feed your family are at stake – not to mention financial independence.

You've got to stop making up stories about yourself and get real about how important marketing is for your business. And you have to cease the endless tinkering on your website, logo, and brand colors (procrasti-branding), instead of simply reaching more people. Yeah, I see you. *Stop tinkering!* Your brand is fine – just *tell* more people about it.

> *'Pretend that every single person you meet has a sign around his or her neck that says, "Make me feel important." Not only will you succeed in sales, you will succeed in life.'*
>
> MARY KAY ASH

Marketing Is a Numbers Game

You might have heard this expression, and every part of you may want to rail against it. You might say things like, 'My customers are special to me, Denise: they aren't just a number!' or 'But I put heart and soul into my marketing.' I'm not saying that's untrue, but you have to be realistic about the amount of marketing needed before potential customers can *experience* your heart and soul for themselves. Was it my fault that nobody bought a second-hand fridge? No. I would have done a great job selling the crap out of it, if only someone, *anyone*, had come in the door.

You're talented and ambitious enough to make a success of your business. You're good enough to hit all your goals. You just don't have enough *eyeballs* on your work right now – simple as that. I have a prescription for you, and it's called *marketing*. Marketing is about connecting with your peeps, so you can love them and help them solve challenges in their lives through your life-changing products.

Here's what marketing is *not* about:

✦ Making money through people's misery or problems.

✦ Bothering or annoying people until they say yes.

✦ Using Neuro-Linguistic Programming (NLP) in an evil way.

✦ Conning people out of their money.

Some of the most beautiful, big-hearted people worry that marketing is some evil form of trickery, but it's not. I often hear entrepreneurs say they don't want or need to learn marketing; they'll 'manifest' the clients instead. Let's reframe marketing right now: marketing *is* manifesting! Manifesting means 'to make real,' and marketing is a pretty quick way of bringing in real clients who will pay you real, spendable money in return. Win-win.

— *Lesson* —

Marketing is how you manifest clients.

Chillpreneur marketing

Marketing doesn't have to be scary. Chillpreneur marketing is just:

1. Sharing what you know, and

2. Making offers.

Did you know that I have an actual marketing degree? I nailed all my marketing subjects and failed everything else because, instead of going to economics and accounting classes, I was president of my campus business club and performing as a professional sports mascot on the side. But even though I have legit marketing credentials, they didn't help in my business until I embraced these two things: sharing and making offers. It's that simple. *Share* your knowledge, expertise, advice, tips, experience, horror stories, mistakes and successes with people. And then, *offer* a solution.

This straightforward, two-step marketing strategy has made me millions of dollars. It's empowered me to live a life of freedom, adventure, abundance and joy (our family values). I've been able to support family members financially, donate to important charities, and fund causes dear to my heart. It's helped me build my dream house, buy new cars, and supported my crystal, candle, and book addictions. Money is awesome. Making money by helping people is even awesomer.

Those two steps are honestly all you need to do, whether your goal is to make millions or just a few extra hundred bucks on the side to help pay the mortgage. It's the same process either way.

That's how I started my Lucky Bitch 'empire,' and that's what I continue to do these days. If you follow me on social media, you'll see that I regularly share what I know about success, money blocks, and other topics, and then I suggest you either buy my book or sign up for one of my courses. My marketing strategy hasn't changed in *years*, and it works incredibly well because I don't overthink it.

Of course, there are nuances, but not as many as you think. You could get caught up in finding the 'perfect' marketing channel or stress about creating the 'perfect' offer, but my advice is just to get started and tweak as you go. Most women are actually great at sharing but terrible at making offers. They have no problem helping people for free. They write great blog posts, give tons of free advice, and will gladly respond to email inquiries that never lead to a sale. But they forget (or are too scared) to tell people they have a solution.

The truth is that people will take and take *and take* if you let them. Some will be thankful and praise you for your generosity, but that's not going to pay your bills. Lots of people will accept your free support and never even thank you. Applause is great, and helping people for free is noble, but you know what's also awesome? *Money in the bank.* You can give the best, most life-changing advice in the world but, without an offer, your potential customers will think 'that's nice' and move on with their lives.

There's no silver-bullet solution to growing your business. Just share what you know and make offers. I know you're scared to put yourself out there. Everyone is. That's not a good enough excuse. The world doesn't owe you a successful business (or life). It's up to you to decide that you're good enough exactly as you are and to show up and be counted.

In this section of the book, I'm going to share with you chill marketing techniques that will make your life easier and your bank account happier. But not one of them will be 'build it, and they will come.' I'm going to get straight with you: this is a skill you need to get moderately good at. Not perfect, just good enough. In most cases, you can even half-ass it and still get great results (honestly). I almost called this book *Lucky Bitch Slap*, because we as women have to get real about the role that marketing plays in our businesses.

> **'A year from now, you'll wish you had started today.'**
> KAREN LAMB

In Oprah style, here's 'what I know for sure' about your business. You'll:

✤ Sabotage yourself (and it will cost you sales).

✤ Feel scared when you ask people for money.

✤ Resist doing the work.

Fear costs you money, time, and freedom – and it's keeping your dreams out of reach. *Hoping* that your potential will be fulfilled won't make it happen. *Hoping* for clients to (physically or metaphorically) walk through the door won't make them come. Blaming yourself for not being perfect isn't the answer. You have to show up and make yourself known to your potential customers.

I'm not going to slap you – this is just a gentle reminder that you don't have to overcomplicate it. Share what you know, and make offers. You can honestly create whatever size business you want with those two skills (however imperfect), and you can change your world for the better. You can make the money you need to fulfill your dreams, and you can help more people than you thought was possible!

Ready? Let's get started!

— CHAPTER 11 —

The 1 Percent Conversion Rule

'When you accept life as it is, you're free.'
RICHARD CARLSON

*H*ere's a marketing truth that will either be depressing as hell, or the most liberating thing you've ever heard. Don't start marketing anything until you 'get' this: *Not everyone is going to buy.*

Yeah, I know. Revolutionary right? Totally worth the cost of this book! But do you know, on average, how many people will actually buy from you during your next marketing campaign, or are you just hoping for the best?

When I see people depressed over their failed launch or crying because their event didn't sell out, I ask, 'What were your conversion statistics? How many people viewed your sales page?' Yeah, okay, I may have failed Statistics 101 in college, but in business I finally realized the power of knowing this stuff. It's helped me be incredibly chill about my results and, in most cases, to be able to predict exactly how many sales (and even refunds) we'll see during a launch.

Mark once asked me to guess the sales figures from our latest marketing campaign, and all I asked was how many people we'd emailed. Knowing that our average email open rate is around 25 percent, our average click-through rate is 10 percent, and the sales conversion is around 1 to 2 percent, I guessed it almost exactly. It's predictable, but Mark was amazed. It was like a party trick! I'm not psychic; I'm just realistic about my sales conversions stats!

This is probably a vast generalization, but I've found that many women have a *huge* mental block around learning about sales conversions. I don't know if it sounds scary, if they think it's too complicated, or something else. But sales conversions, like gravity, are a truth that you just can't ignore. Not everyone will buy, and your sales results will follow a regular statistical pattern. Don't believe me? Track your next marketing campaign, and then read this section of the book again. Virgos are rarely wrong!

Once I overcame my own resistance to tracking statistics, it was simple: just calculate how many people visited the sales page versus how many people bought from you. Once you know, it's not scary, it's actually fun, because you can set goals that you can achieve and have actual data you can use (instead of a vague, unexplained feeling that you're a loser).

The 1 Percent Conversion Rule Explained

On average, only 1 to 2 percent of people who see your sales page will buy. So, if you get 100 visitors to your page and only one sale, you're actually right on track. The bigger your numbers get, the more that statistic will play out. You might get 100 visitors, no sales, and be like, 'Hey Denise, where's my money?' But that 1 percent conversion might not kick in until you've had at least 1,000 people view your sales page. Either way, it's not personal: it's just the numbers playing out.

Now, 1 percent conversion is a good rule of thumb for a regular marketing campaign, but you *can* get higher conversions depending on *how* you're selling. Using a more high-touch approach like selling over the phone (for example, converting prospective clients from a free consult to a paid package), you could convert anything from 25 to 75 percent, depending on your skill and how well you pre-screen your potential clients. Selling from the stage to a cold audience could lead to an average conversion rate of 5 to 15 percent of the room. I have friends who've achieved a 60 to 80 percent conversion rate because of how well they pre-screened their audience.

But for any mass marketing campaign such as advertising (online and in print), email marketing, or direct response (such as letters or postcards), you're looking at 1 to 2 percent of customers who will buy.

Is that sobering? Scary? Daunting? I'm sorry about that, but I honestly hope it feels empowering because it gives you actual information about what it will take to hit your sales targets. Even though it sounds like more work to be aware of it, having a realistic barometer of success helps you be more chill and accepting of reality (and to take that reality less personally).

I'm often asked: can you beat the stats by being better than your competitors – for example, by having a sexier sales page, killer bonuses, or launching when Mercury isn't retrograde? Yes and no. Look at these list-size/conversion-rate numbers for some of my first few launches:

List size	Sales	Conversion rate
2,466	14	0.57 percent
3,461	42	1.21 percent
4,436	44	0.99 percent
5,275	42	0.80 percent
7,236	76	1.05 percent

Remember: 1 percent is a *good* conversion rate. I didn't always make it. You might think that because I'm a fancy internet millionaire with a massive newsletter list, my statistics must be better, but they aren't. My last launch converted at 1.12 percent with a list of around 100,000 people. You could argue that I'm way smarter about marketing now than when I started out, but I can't beat the stats! In fact, my sales conversion rate actually went *down* when I made my sales page 'too sexy' and professional. Simple is best.

EXERCISE: LEARN YOUR STATISTICS

In your journal, or in a conversation with an entrepreneurial friend, answer these questions:

- What's the average conversion statistic for my industry?
- What are my past results?
- What do I need to do to be able to handle more customers?
- How many potential customers do I need to achieve my next sales goal?

Why the 1 Percent Rule Is a Good Thing

Be thankful for the 1 percent conversion rule: the universe is giving you what you can handle right now. That's why only a handful of people tend to buy your first product, which is exactly what happened with my Raw Brides Transformation Plan wedding weight-loss course back in 2009. I had one customer.

Like most people starting out, you probably don't have robust procedures in place to deal with a massive influx of new customers who have a million questions, who inevitably lose their passwords (more than once), need hand-holding to access your materials, and find broken links or typos in them when they do (been there!)

As your potential customer base grows, so does your ability to handle volume. New things, like your first refund request or a customer who defaults on a payment, can send you into a tizzy because you don't have procedures in place to deal with them. And you make mistakes because you're learning on the job. I've seen unicorns (very rare outliers) somehow beat the statistics and smash their sales targets, then crash and burn because they don't have the capacity, team, or systems to realistically serve that many people.

Have you heard of the Passion Planners, founded by Angelia Trinidad? In 2014, Angelia was shipping and packing planners out of her garage, printing out labels, and driving to the post office herself. That year, she shipped 2,147 planners, which was an incredible achievement. The following year, her crowdfunding campaign went viral and raised more than $650,000 from more than 23,000 customers (her goal was $10,000). That's suddenly a lot of planners for one person to fulfill.

Angelia just wasn't equipped to pack and ship 3,000 planners *a day* by herself, especially when port strikes that were entirely out of her control held up shipping, making her customers *furious*. Suddenly, she was handling thousands of customer service complaints, tweets, texts and bad nationwide P.R.,[1] not to mention dealing with suppliers, finding a new warehouse, hiring (and training) new staff to do the physical packing, and buying a van to deal with deliveries to the post office.

Talk about firefighting! She was making up procedures and policies minute by minute in response to all the problems and requests for refunds. She barely slept for months. Most people would crumble after such an experience, but Angelia survived and is still going strong. (I buy a planner whenever they issue one in turquoise!)

Here's the lesson: it's okay to build your company steadily and consciously, so don't feel bad if your first (or last) campaign wasn't as successful as you wanted. As you can see, growing too fast can bring trouble. Seriously, if you only got a couple of customers in your first marketing launch, *you are a huge success*. You overcame all that resistance, tech problems, and money blocks, and someone *paid you to do it.* Even if you had no customers, you still created something, and it can be refined and improved for next time.

Trust me: you don't always *want* a ton of customers when you're not ready to handle them. There will be times when you have to grow faster than others (like for example when Sara Blakely got a call saying that her new product, Spanx, was going to be on Oprah's Favorite Things show), but it's better to make your mistakes when there aren't too many people watching. Build a secure container, so you can handle more people in the future. I believe the 1 percent conversion rule saves us from massive stress by pacing our success so it's more manageable. Thanks universe!

— *Lesson* —

Having a 1 percent conversion rate isn't failure. It's success, so celebrate!

CHAPTER 12

Cat Charming and Internet Dating

'When you don't close a sale, open a relationship.'
PATRICIA FRIPP

*B*efore you get into the nitty-gritty of marketing techniques, you have to change your mindset about yourself as a salesperson. Everyone wants sales (and money), but *nobody* wants to be a salesperson, especially those who see their work as art or who help people transform their lives. Selling might feel dirty, and others might accuse you of 'selling out' just by putting a price tag on your services. I don't consider myself a salesperson either, even though I've sold more than 7 million dollars' worth of online courses. I consider myself more of a cat charmer.

Let me explain. I love cats, but you know how cats are: they don't always love you back. Have you ever tried to coax your cat out from under the couch when it doesn't want to come? Impossible! But I have a foolproof way of getting any cat to fall in love with me. It's easy. I sit near it (but not too close), and then I pretend I'm petting an imaginary cat. I 'speak' to it in cat talk and scratch it behind its imaginary ears.

The real cat can't stand it and, within a minute, comes over and begs for the same attention. It works every time. Same with dogs. Have you ever tried to chase a dog that doesn't want to be caught? It's frustrating. But if you give up and lie down on the grass, it can't help itself: it'll run over and lick your face.

Reminder: find the path of least resistance.

My marketing philosophy is simple: 'I'm just going to do my thing over here, and I'm having a great time. Do you want to join me? Cool either way!' I'm not saying that clients will rush over and lick your face, but this is way more fun that trying too hard to make everyone like you.

Liking myself regardless of what other people think of me is honestly my only personal development tool these days. That and my simple marketing strategy – share and make offers – seem to be a lucrative combination! My customers figure that, if I'm that chill about my work, it must be *really* good!

Have you noticed that, when you feel really desperate, opportunities seem to dry up? They say the best time to look for a new job is when you already have one, rather than when you really *need* one. I'm sure the same goes for dating or anything else you want. Desperation isn't sexy. Being unattached doesn't mean doing nothing. *You* have to believe you have something to offer your clients before *they* will believe it.

When I had a small list for my newsletter, I wrote it as if thousands of people were reading it, and that eventually came true. When I hosted my first few webinars (with zero attendees), I pretended there were thousands listening, and eventually there were. Again, the reason I can be so chill about sales is because:

❖ I understand my sales conversion numbers.

- I know that some people want what I have to offer, and some people don't.
- I don't take rejection personally because I believe in what I do.
- I like myself either way.

'Some will, some won't. So what? Someone else is waiting.'
JACK CANFIELD

If you get enough people in a room, or on the telephone, and make an offer, you'll make sales eventually. But if you're shouting into the void or spending all your time tweaking your website instead of marketing your offers, you'll never hit your income targets.

Why Marketing Is Like Internet Dating

I've always been a 'path of least resistance' girl, so when I wanted to find a partner, I figured that internet dating was the fastest way to meet a lot of people quickly. I decided to treat dating like a marketing campaign and even wrote my marketing thesis on internet dating (which my professors thought was super-dumb); I also had a short-lived dating course and book (major shiny object).

The most significant mistake people make in both internet dating and marketing their business is being too passive. They wait for customers to walk in the door, like me at my stepdad's white goods store. Big mistake. Having a profile on a dating website doesn't mean you'll automatically find your soulmate – just like having an Etsy store doesn't mean your product will sell itself. You have to be proactive and sell yourself.

Another big mistake is believing in scarcity. If you compare yourself to others whom you perceive as 'better,' you'll let doubt creep in and think there's no place for you. Remember, there's enough pie for everyone. A third mistake is to get scared about rejection. Hearing no from potential customers sucks, but you have to put yourself out there to gain anything good in life.

Before I started my 'internet dating formula' experiment, I got really specific about my goals and target audience. I created a list of the traits I wanted in a partner and separated it into 'preferences' and 'deal-breakers' (for example, I didn't want a partner who smoked cigarettes, but I wasn't too bothered about height). My dating profile was like a mini-sales page to pre-screen my potential dates. I chose my photos carefully and experimented with my 'sales copy,' so I stood out and seemed interesting enough for a second look.

Once I got clear on my target, I put out some 'bait,' with an introductory private message to 100 suitable guys. I didn't sit and agonize over each profile, wondering what our future children would look like. I just scanned their profiles and, as long as they roughly fit my preferences and deal-breakers lists, they got a copy-and-pasted private message in which I introduced myself.

Reaching out to customers is where most women get stuck with marketing. You might need to get on the phone with 100 potential customers before you hear 'yes,' or it might be 10. But a lot of people get freaked out at the first 'no' and stop asking. In marketing speak, this is called a funnel: you might need to contact a lot of people before a few winners shake out at the bottom. It isn't callous or impersonal – it's just what it takes to find the right 'customers', and the sooner you can accept it, the quicker you'll become chill about it.

The 10,000 Hours Rule

Malcolm Gladwell's book *Outliers: The Story of Success* says that, once you get to 10,000 hours of practice in any field, you'll master it. If you want to be an elite-level violinist or an Olympic gold medalist, for example, you probably need at least 10,000 hours of practice.

But in the real world? Being able to run a business that supports yourself, your family, and your goals doesn't need that level of mastery.

It also perpetuates the Wonder Woman/Smurfette/Highlander theory I mentioned earlier. You don't have to be that special, or 'The One,' to be successful in business. Any number of entrepreneurs can be successful, there's lots of room at the top, and last I checked, there's no gold medal to compete for.

Because we're Chillpreneurs and want to follow an easier path, let's call it the '100-hour rule.' Contact 100 customers or film 100 videos, and you're going to see massive improvement and results. It probably doesn't even take that much effort. Host 10 webinars, and you'll be ahead of 99 percent of entrepreneurs who are too scared to do even one! Okay – let's call it the '1-hour rule,' because starting is better than nothing!

> *'New mantra for work that I'm worried is beyond me:*
> *"Anything I come up with is literally better than nothing."'*
>
> MARSHA SHANDUR

If you start out thinking that you'll have to contact thousands of people before you make any money, you'll probably talk yourself out of it! Start with one newsletter. Start with one sentence in your book: *just take action.*

Back to internet dating: I copy-and-pasted an identical introductory message to 100 guys, so I was casting my net quite wide. Yes, this takes work, but you don't get results by just showing up and doing the bare minimum. Nobody is going to visit your website if you don't market yourself a little. Nobody is going to know what you do if you hide yourself. I got about 25 responses, same as my newsletter open rate! The 75 guys who 'ignored' me? Maybe not interested, didn't like my photo, or didn't see my message that day. For whatever reason, there wasn't a match. Some people just won't be into you.

Here's another thing to look forward to: when you send out an email, some people will unsubscribe. Some will even write back and tell you why (in some cases in a nasty way). It's very, *very* predictable.

Turn notifications off, so you don't get unsubscribe reports. It's not useful for you to fixate on that number. Unsubscribers aren't your people, and they've self-selected out. You want a 100 percent open rate and no unsubscribes? Great. Just delete everyone from your newsletter list and keep your biggest fan (who might be your mother)! You won't have any customers, but you'll never get hurt feelings.

I started a conversation with the 25 guys who replied to my message, to see if we had anything in common. This is called 'nurturing your audience' and doesn't necessarily lead directly into a sale, any more than a response on a dating site leads to a wedding the next day. For my business, I build up a 'know, like, and trust' factor by producing weekly content, giving out free tips on social media, and otherwise being of service to my audience. That's just like having a casual conversation, and again, people will self-select out.

Of those 25 guys, I eventually invited about 10 on a 'mini-date' for a casual game of pool and a beer. I even batched these meet-ups at 6 and 8 p.m. with different guys. That's dating Virgo style: practical, efficient, and unemotional! I'm a big fan of batching – grouping similar tasks together – in life and business. Batch all your marketing activities if you can; record several videos when you have good hair and makeup; spend a day writing articles for the month ahead; or make all your sales calls back to back when you're in the groove. Take advantage of energy bursts! (More on batching later.)

Pre-Screening Your Customers

In marketing, as in dating, pre-screening is essential. It's really uncomfortable being stuck on a sales call with someone you already know isn't going to be a good customer for you. It makes you both feel like losers and is a massive waste of time and energy. Don't be afraid to tell customers what you're looking for in a perfect match, so they can self-select out of your marketing funnel. If I were ever single again, I'd get my assistant to pre-screen potential dates for me.

A great example of elegant pre-screening is Kathryn Hocking's sales page for her VIP launch management services.[1] She helps people determine whether they are a match for what she offers by asking them these questions:

❖ Do you feel alone in your business, like you are the only one holding the reins?

❖ Have you got great team members and providers, but still feel like it's all down to you to make sure things happen?

❖ Do you want to be able to stay directly in your zone of genius – as the figurehead of your brand – engaging and serving your community?

❖ Are you ready for the next level of 'going pro' in your business – bringing on a project manager, launch manager, or new program development manager?

She then helps those who *aren't* a match for what she offers recognize themselves as such, saying my services aren't for you if:

❖ You are struggling to pay your bills, and you are hoping this will save you.

❖ You don't already have an established list, social media following, and proven success with online products, programs, or one-to-one services.

❖ You don't have any other support team members – I work best when I can maximize the team you already have and fill the gaps as needed.

❖ You are not willing to invest in a suitable budget for a launch or new product development. I can work with varying budgets, but generally, we will need some web and graphic design, copywriting, and advertising budget in addition to my services.

If Kathryn didn't pre-qualify her audience, she'd spend time on the phone with people who have zero marketing budget, team, or customer list. That's stressful for both parties. This is why casting your net wide at the start is so important. You don't want to feel desperate for everyone to say yes, or sign up a non-ideal client despite very obvious red flags. Been there, done that, *never again*.

— *Lesson* —

Customers don't want to be caught:
they want to be courted.

Now, you might be curious about how my dating story ends. Did I find the love of my life (my hubby Mark) through this process? Yes and no. First up, look at the statistics again: 100 dating messages, 25 potentials, 10 mini-dates. That follows, almost exactly, my marketing conversion statistics.

Two of the mini-dates ended up being really great potential partners whom I dated casually, but then I met Mark through a work thing, and it was love at (almost) first sight. So, does that disprove the 1 percent rule? No. From a Law of Attraction perspective, I was 'open for business' to find a partner. You'll never know where that 1 percent will come from unless you take action to put yourself out there. Knock on a dozen doors, and the universe will knock on 1,000 for you.

I can't resist stretching this analogy one step further. When you find your 'perfect match,' the work doesn't end there. Partnerships take work (customer service), you might decide to grow your family (hire staff), or need a bigger house and car (upgrade your systems). You might redefine your preferences and deal-breakers (your target market might change over time), and some partnerships might even end in divorce (refund requests). But my point is, whether it's business or love, you've got to get in the game!

EXERCISE: BECOMING
MORE ATTRACTIVE TO YOUR CLIENTS

In your journal or in a conversation with an entrepreneurial friend, answer these questions:

- Am I cat charming my customers?
- How can I get more eyeballs on my business (or butts in seats)?
- Can I pre-screen my customers better? How?
- What can I learn for my business from Denise's dating formula?

CHAPTER 13

Show Up, Be Seen, and Be Heard

'I have never worked a day in my life without selling. If I believe in something, I sell it, and I sell it hard.'

ESTÉE LAUDER

L et's recap on my super-complicated, two-step millionaire marketing formula:

1. Share what you know, and

2. Make offers.

Before we start, a reminder: the basics work, but only if you work them. Some people second-guess the basics because they're so damned unsexy. They want a silver-bullet solution instead. Others avoid them as a form of rebellion ('If *everyone* is doing it, I'll do the *opposite!*'), even if that sabotages their business.

Nobody wants to hear this, but the way I grew my business to six and then seven figures, was consistency, *not* perfection. I'm not super-organized, I don't have superior planning skills, and I don't have a solid marketing strategy. Nope. I've half-assed my way to a successful business, but I've half-assed *consistently*! I show up even when I'm second-guessing it. Just get on with it.

In this chapter, we'll cover the 'sharing' part of your very simple marketing strategy; after all, what is marketing if not just sharing what you're passionate about? First, let's cover some frequently asked questions about marketing.

How Do I Build My Marketing List?

'Money doesn't grow on trees; it grows in your list!'
NATALIE SISSON

One of the truisms of marketing is that the money is in your list. In this case, your list is your customer database, your newsletter subscribers, and your social media following. These are people who are interested in your business and in how you can help them.

If 'list' feels too impersonal to you, give your community a name! Lady Gaga has 'Little Monsters.' Nicki Minaj has 'Barbz.' And I have 'Lucky Bees.' Whatever you call them, your people are your gold. They aren't just the source of your income – they're how you can create loyalty and a big movement.

You might be thinking, *If 1 percent is a good conversion rate, and I have fewer than 100 people in my community, I'm doomed.'* Not true! But building an audience should be a major marketing priority for you. I don't want to brag, but I have a *pretty* big list (wink, wink), and I can tell you from experience that it's easier to build a Chillpreneur business when you have a lot more people to market to. Size *does* matter if you want to do less work and make more money, especially with passive income products.

My Lucky Bee community has grown slowly and consistently over many years and, for a long time, I didn't spend any money on advertising, just my time and energy. My best list-building tip is to give, give, and give some more, with a mindset of 'people want to hear from me' and 'I have something valuable to share.' Stop thinking you're bothering people by sharing your knowledge with them. Remember: you don't have to be the über-expert. People want to hear *your* perspective and experience, so give it to them! Give away free resources, show the results from your last marketing campaign, tell an embarrassing story about one of your biggest business or life mistakes, show how you create your artwork, give tips and tricks that you've learned along the way, or share internal resources that save you time. The only caveat is that it has to be relevant to your business and useful to your target market.

Then *ask*: ask for an email address in return, ask for a follow on social media, and (most importantly) ask for *permission* to contact them again! Nurture that community with regular material to develop your 'know, like, and trust' factor and then, when you have something for sale, ask for the sale!

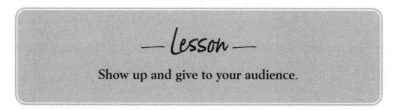

— *Lesson* —

Show up and give to your audience.

Don't overthink this. Your free content has to be useful enough for people to take the next step to becoming part of your community (either as a subscriber or follower). Always find the path of least resistance and create what's easiest for you, instead of procrastinating and waiting for the 'perfect' marketing idea.

Because I'm passionate about consistency, I've had the discipline of creating something new every week for years. And here's the thing: you never know what will resonate with your audience. I've spent hours agonizing over a blog post, only to hear... nothing... in return. Other weeks, I've dashed something out before my newsletter deadline, and people loved it! That's why you have to show up regularly if you want to build your audience consistently.

Tips for Creating Awesome Content

✦ **Remember the basics**. In my case that means 'What is a money block?' Don't forget that people are looking for the basics, so take them step by step, even if it feels obvious to you. The frequently asked questions you get via email or social media can give you ideas. Bonus: you can point new people to existing content instead of repeating yourself constantly!

✦ **Be useful**. Don't share for the sake of it. How does what you share help your audience? Does it solve a relevant problem? Point people toward resources, hacks, or shortcuts. It's okay to make these affiliate links and make some commission in the process (just disclose it). If you've created a tool for your business, share it with your audience.

✦ **Be inspirational**. People love to see transformations, so show before-and-afters of yourself and your clients. This works well for designers, weight-loss coaches, stylists, and even artists (show the progression, too). Remember: a picture is worth a thousand words.

✦ **Be real**. How do you make your artwork? Organize your cupboard? Make your kids' school lunches or create videos on the fly? People are curious (and nosy). You don't have to show your audience everything (keep it relevant), but in my experience, behind-the-scenes content builds trust and relationships with your audience more quickly than anything else.

✤ **Don't be afraid of giving all your best secrets away in your free content**. The more value you give, the more people will want to work with you! The point of sharing is to develop strong relationships so that, when the time is right, your customers will line up to give you money!

✤ **Search online for content ideas**. You'll find lots out there. That way, you'll never run out of things to talk about (and if you do, you might be in the wrong business!)

✤ **Build community**. If you can't find the place where your peeps gather in real life or online, create it. Become the leader you're looking for and create a community that gives people a sense of belonging. When you compare the words 'email list' or 'followers' to the word 'community,' which feels better – for you *and* the people you serve? People want to feel like they belong, not that they are a cash cow for you. I don't just send messages to my list or post for my followers – I built a community, and I watch with pride as members of that community *support each other*.

EXERCISE: CONTENT IDEAS

In your journal, or in a conversation with an entrepreneurial friend, answer these questions:

• What knowledge can I share with my audience?

• What type of content would be the easiest for me to create?

• How would I like to turn my 'list' into a community? Is there a cool name we can call ourselves?

What's the Best Marketing Tool?

I'm not going to recommend a particular marketing tool, social media platform, or technology here, because they change so often. By the time you read this, we could be hologramming into each other's living rooms! The core of marketing is unchanging: get your message out there. Just choose the medium that works best for you and your audience.

Ignore coaches or marketing gurus who tell you that you can market only in one way. I once interviewed with a coach who told me that I had to go to every networking event within three hours of my house. When I told her I wanted a more online model because a) I'm an introvert, b) I have young children, and c) people, ew, she said, 'Online? But how would you get clients?' Needless to say, I didn't hire her. There are easier ways (for me) to make money.

You can choose the most comfortable and enjoyable marketing strategies for you. If you don't want to be on camera, you can write blogs or start a podcast. If you love spontaneity, you can do livestreams whenever you feel like it. If you're a former high-school thespian, you can confidently create silly or funny videos. But if you prefer face-to-face work, you can make networking and public speaking a major part of your marketing strategy. Respect your preferences and personality: you'll likely be more consistent than you would be if you followed the latest sexy marketing fad or forced yourself into doing something 'everyone else' is doing.

As an introvert, I like marketing in a way that requires minimal contact with other humans. I only speak on stages a few times a year; I hate traditional networking events; and I have to psych myself up to attend launch parties (even my own!) I like telling stories, so I love being interviewed on audio podcasts (because I don't have to wear a bra or makeup!) My videos and interviews can go out to thousands of people (who I don't have to meet in person), so I choose the most leveraged, easy way for me to reach as many people as possible. Remember: the key is knowing your personality.

> — *Lesson* —
>
> **Get your message out to more people in whatever way feels good to you.**

You don't have to do *all the things*. Some marketing platforms won't resonate with you, and that's okay. Start by focusing on the easiest medium for you – otherwise, you might never start! Give yourself permission to start something new and easy and drop something hard or boring. Just because others are doing it, doesn't mean it's right for you!

EXERCISE: MARKETING IDEAS

In your journal, or in conversation with an entrepreneurial friend, answer these questions:

- What's the most natural way for me to market (writing, audio, video, speaking, or networking)?
- What's something new I'd love to make for my audience?
- What would I like to drop from my marketing?
- If I had to choose just one marketing medium, what would it be?

How Often Should I Contact My Audience?

*'People talk about perfect timing, but I think
everything is perfect in its moment.'*

EDDIE HUANG

You know those 'friends' who pop back into your life every time they want something? Yeah, don't be that kind of marketer. You've got to show up consistently and give a lot of value between sales campaigns.

According to the Marketing Rule of 7 (which originated in the 1930s), people need to hear a message *at least* seven times before they act on it.[1] In some ways that's easier to do in the digital age but also harder because there's *so much information*. I've heard that the number of contacts needed to lead people to action has increased, which wouldn't surprise me – we're bombarded with media that didn't exist in the 1930s.

A good rule of thumb for the frequency of contacting your audience could be:

◈ **A daily-ish presence on social media**. For example, a photo, inspirational quote, or a resource such as an article or book.

◈ **A weekly in-depth share**. For example, a helpful newsletter, article, podcast, resource, or video.

◈ **A monthly training**. For example, a live webinar to share your expertise and remind people how to work with you.

◈ **A quarterly launch**. For example, something new or a special offer on something that already exists.

A lot of woo-woo and spiritual entrepreneurs ask me about 'divine timing,' like, 'Is there a perfect time to launch my website or book?' or 'What's the best day of the week to send out my newsletter?' Here's my philosophy: *The day you do it is your lucky day.*

Yes, I'll admit that I look at my horoscope to get good launch dates, but not as an excuse to procrastinate or wait for the stars to align before I take action. If you can muster the energy only to launch on a particular day, go with that. Don't psych yourself out looking for the perfect time to send your newsletter. Pick a date and time and send it out – you can always change it. I've met many entrepreneurs who have done nothing for years for fear of getting it wrong. Sometimes, you just have to launch and see what happens!

> *'Repetition makes reputation and*
> *reputation makes customers.'*
>
> ELIZABETH ARDEN

More Timing Tips

✦ **Check for clashes.** Don't launch on the night of a presidential election or a major holiday weekend (ask me how I know). It takes only a few minutes to check dates, and there might be a festival or a national or international day that's actually better for sending promotions related to your business.

✦ **Respect your target market.** We used to close promotions at midnight, until I realized that my target market was probably in bed! The midnight deadline comes from the male-dominated internet marketing world, which is probably perfect if your target market is a 20-something childless, male entrepreneur. Ours meant that my team had to stay up late making sure everything was okay. If something doesn't work for your customers (or you), go against what the gurus tell you. You know your customers best.

✦ **Be kind to yourself.** Don't launch on your birthday, unless you want to ruin your day, and although life happens, think twice about launching if you know you won't have childcare or your partner is away (I've done both and it can be done, but isn't the easiest!)

Consistency is so much more important than finding the perfect timing. Why? Social media is like a digital river. You never know if the people you want to reach will be standing on the bank when your tweet, email, or post flows by. Become a reliable presence in people's lives, and they'll get excited to buy from you when the time comes.

> *'Patience doesn't mean making a pact with the devil*
> *of denial, ignoring our emotions and aspirations.*
> *It means being wholeheartedly engaged in the*
> *process that's unfolding, rather than ripping open*
> *a budding flower or demanding a caterpillar hurry*
> *up and get that chrysalis stage over with.'*
>
> SHARON SALZBERG

Bonus Million-Dollar Marketing Tips

You want some *advanced* strategies? Okay, here they are: share *more* and make *more* offers. I'm only kinda kidding – it really is that basic. But if you insist, here are some nuances that have really helped me.

Don't Reinvent the Wheel

Writer and comedian Judd Apatow recommends that stand-up comedians stick to 80 percent tried-and-true material that they *know* people will laugh at, and try out new content only 20 percent of the time. I saw Bette Midler's show in Vegas, during which she said, 'I've been telling the same jokes for 30 years. But you keep laughing, so I keep telling them!' And she was right – I laughed my ass off!

Listen to the superstars and chill out. You don't have to reinvent everything. I've been teaching money mindset for several years now, and let's be honest: I'm saying the same things over and over in slightly different ways from slightly different perspectives.

Most entrepreneurs assume that everything has to be 100 percent new or it doesn't count. But don't assume that everyone has seen *everything* you've created (remember the river). It's okay to repurpose older content because it will be new to a lot of your audience (especially if you've grown your business recently) and your loyal customers won't mind. I tell the same stories on stage all the time (just like Bette Midler)! But even my oldest clients tell me they loved hearing a message reinforced or appreciated finding a new nugget of wisdom in an old lesson.

While your audience is small, you might develop content that few people will see, but consider it an apprenticeship. Every time you put something out there, you're becoming a better writer, podcaster, or video producer. Keep practicing! The blog posts, videos, and podcasts you create will accumulate and create a library of media that your growing audience can discover any time.

Not Everything Is Your Job

Remember: being the 'go-to' girl isn't super-fun or lucrative. It's tempting to solve everyone's problems but knowing what's out of scope for your marketing is essential. Give yourself some 'content rules,' so you can catch yourself before you go too off-topic. I steer clear of the following: how-to advice – I don't usually give detailed information about *how* to make more money; instead, I stick to the mindset behind it; financial advice or accounting (I'm not qualified to give that, anyway); technical business advice – don't ask me about the best software to use for anything!

Narrowing your scope might mean killing some of your old or existing content. I had to delete all my old blog posts about random off-topic things. I unpublished some of my old books, including an e-book called *Planning a Green and Ethical Wedding*. Hardly anyone bought it, but it still came up in online searches, which diluted my message. Get focused, and watch your audience grow. Be everything to everyone, and you'll never stand out in a crowded market.

— *Lesson* —

Get focused about what you do and don't offer.

Batch and Schedule

If you follow me on social media, you might think I work 24/7. I really don't. The truth is that I work *way less* now than I did several years ago, and I make a ton more money. I seem way more 'on' than I actually am, even when I'm doing 'life stuff' like being on holidays or having my babies, because a lot of my marketing is batched and automated. I once sat down at my computer and created 200 affirmation images for my website; I was inspired (and to be honest, procrastinating something else), but that was over a year's worth of content for my social media. When you're in a groove, keep going!

When I'm pregnant, I batch video content ahead of time, so I'm not missed during my maternity leave. I once even hired a studio for three days and created a year's worth of videos because I knew I had a new book to write and wanted to conserve my energy that year but still serve my community with fresh weekly content. Batching will change your life and free up so much time for you. It also really focuses your marketing on what's important. When you're clear on your audience and your topic (and on what's out of scope), it's really easy to brainstorm a lot of potential marketing ideas.

Batching also saves you a lot of money if you're outsourcing because it gives you economy of scale. It's cheaper to give your graphic designer 20 similar jobs to do at the same time than it is to send the work out piecemeal over several months. Then, when you have a lot of content, you can schedule it using free or low-cost software, so your marketing is consistent without you having to think about it. You can schedule things to go out automatically on a daily, weekly, or monthly basis.

— *Lesson* —

You don't have to be 'on' 24/7. Embrace batching and automation, so you can chill a bit and not have to work so hard.

The concept is simple but mindset around batching is fascinating. You may resist it because it feels inauthentic to you. Shouldn't you just share when you *feel* like it? My answer is: if I'd waited until I 'felt like it,' I wouldn't have a business, let alone a financially successful one. The idea of a regular marketing schedule might sound exhausting, but not if you embrace the power of technology for scheduling and batching.

Plus, here's the thing: it's not about you. As long as your marketing was authentic when you *created* it, it's none of your business when your audience *consumes it*. It might actually come at the perfect time for them, even if it's 'old news' to you.

My only caveat is that, in my experience, it's best not to batch more than six months in advance. Any more than that and your branding or message might feel a bit stale. I once lost a ton of weight and cut my hair after filming 60 videos, and they annoyed me every time I saw them because they felt so out of date. Find your happy medium!

Ideas for batching

✤ Instead of responding to emails all day, set aside time in the morning and afternoon.

✤ If you're creating graphics for your website, create a template and create multiple graphics at the same time.

✤ If you're going to do your hair and makeup, record four videos instead of just one. Or, if you're going to set up your audio equipment, interview multiple podcast guests on the same day.

✤ Batch your client-facing days instead of spreading them out through the week, so you have more time for marketing or for coming up with new ideas.

✤ Write all your newsletter content for the month ahead.

Make People Feel Less Alone

The best thing about the internet now is realizing that you're not alone. Sharing helps people feel understood and assures them that you have similar problems in common – or that you did until you solved those problems in a way that enables you to help them. Entrepreneurs have a huge advantage over big companies because we can be more personal in our marketing and create intimate relationships with our clients.

When I started my business, I realized the blog posts that got the most traction were ones in which I simply told the truth. *My* truth. When I did that, without shame or embellishment, people *loved* it. For example, I posted a picture of me using hair removal crème on my mustache. People said, 'Oh Denise, you're so funny!' I wasn't trying to be funny, and it had nothing to do with money, but I wanted to be honest and show that my life isn't all hammocks on the beach, *because it's not.*

Nobody has a perfect life but, for some reason, we all fear that we're not perfect enough and that, if our audience saw the 'real us,' they wouldn't like us anymore. The way to overcome this is what I call my 'Hairy Toes Strategy' (HTS). When I was younger, I honestly thought I was the only person in the world to have 'unladylike' hair on my toes. It didn't help that I had lots of friends who only seemed to wax the peach fuzz off their legs once a year.

If I'd had a mentor who mentioned that she had hairy toes too, or even had a stray pimple occasionally, I wouldn't have felt like there was something wrong with me all the time. I love working with people who show me their real lives, warts and all. There's something so compelling about showing up and being who you are. Maybe you feel that your accent disqualifies you for success in the business world, or you're worried that, if you disclosed your infertility journey, a physical disability or mental illness, your audience would reject you or think you're 'unprofessional.'

Show people they're not alone. There are people waiting for a leader who looks exactly like *you*. Someone who has your background and has experienced the challenges you've faced. If you're sick of being the only person like you in your industry, talk about it! Have you faced challenges and discrimination? Share it openly. I guarantee you won't be the only one.

I'm not saying that you should turn your whole life into a business. It's okay to take space and privacy for yourself and not share everything, but your very existence might be challenging the norms of your industry. Showing full-length photos of yourself or making videos might be an act of bravery that inspires others to do the same. Being honest about your challenges might be revolutionary for your audience to hear.

There's so much power in talking about taboo topics. Your voice might be the one that tips a whole industry into a new phase! The maker of Icon pee-proof undies (for light bladder leakage) is a company that has changed an industry from an embarrassing secret to a fact of life for a lot of women. One of the first things you see on its website is, 'Yup, it happens to 1 in 3 women, from spring chickens to silver foxes.'[2] My first thought was, *Wow, thank you! I kind of felt like I was the only one.*

Icon doesn't wrap the problem up in vague, flowery language (tampon companies, I'm looking at you). It injects some humor into its marketing – you can join its 'VIPee list,' and there's a 'Dribble Diaries' feature on its blog. It's not crude or crass, it's honest, and it's so freaking reassuring! The owners of Icon created a movement because they were unafraid to tell the truth about a very common problem. And the company's marketing shows women of all shapes, ages, sizes, and colors too.

I'm not saying you need to quit your business and start a hairy toes blog, and you don't have to share anything you're not comfortable with. All I'm saying is: don't be afraid to be genuinely yourself. Will you get criticism for it? Yes, probably. There could be someone who says, 'I can't believe you're talking about this!' Or someone who thinks you're tacky, bragging, or even being crude. But the overwhelming majority of people will thank you. And that little piece of your heart that's terrified of being rejected, shunned, or unlovable if people saw the 'real you' will be comforted and reassured. That's how you become a leader.

Yes, it might take time to grow your audience – everyone starts from zero. But remind yourself that even the 'popular girls' in your industry have probably been slogging it out for some time, including me. I'm not any smarter and definitely not more hardworking than most. I've just been stubbornly consistent and persistent. Show up and share with your community. That's what it takes.

— *Lesson* —

There's no secret, and there are no silver bullets. Show up, be consistent, and share.

CHAPTER 14

Make Offers, Make Money

*'Success is not an accident; it's something
we have to create on purpose.'*

CARRIE GREEN

The reason I'm so passionate about helping women make more money is independence. Making money for yourself will change your life and start a ripple effect throughout your world.

Nobody is responsible for making money in your business except *you*. It sounds obvious, but to make more money, you have to *ask* for it. You need something for people to buy and an easy way for them to give you money. But I'll admit that asking for money (especially in exchange for something that you love) is going to feel scary, and this is when your money blocks will probably have to be revisited.

Even if you feel you've cleared your money blocks, there are times when they (or entirely new ones) will come up. When people tell me they don't have any money blocks, I often say, 'Oh, you don't? Then launch something in your business. You'll see them soon enough!' But don't worry. Like everything in this book, this is about finding the path of least resistance and making it easy for your customers to buy from you. Don't overcomplicate it. You don't need everyone in the world to be your client – just some people!

Understand Why People Buy

> *'People don't buy for logical reasons.*
> *They buy for emotional reasons.'*
> ZIG ZIGLAR

I'm with Zig on that one. Think of some of your biggest purchases – were they logical, or emotional? Heck, I've bought entire *houses* for emotional reasons (and once because I was nine months pregnant and nesting). And I bought an unrenovated 1974 VW Kombi van because it was pretty.

What if your business isn't the 'impulse purchase' kind? What makes people buy things for their business or themselves when they don't 'need' them? People are motivated by a very clear answer to the question 'What's in it for me?' For your customers to see the value in what you do, your offer has to tap into specific universal desires. Otherwise, you'll get frustrated when people keep saying no to you. It's not *you* (or your product) that's the problem: you just haven't shown them the value.

I see way too much wishy-washy marketing because women feel uncomfortable tapping into these universal desires. I get it. I've prided myself on very chill, non-pushy marketing techniques over the years, but I can't deny the power of knowing what customers want (and giving it to them). Even the words 'marketing strategy' might make you feel like there's an ulterior motive, and asking for the sale might feel pushy. But when you tap into specific desires ethically, you're just telling people exactly how you can help them. Give them what they want!

Many women feel it's unethical or exploitative to 'trigger' other people with sales techniques. But there's a difference between negative and positive triggering. I hate marketing that preys on people's fears or desperation. Tapping into people's desires is the opposite: it reminds them of their goals and gets them excited and optimistic about changing their lives. It's important to use your power of persuasion for good. I see so many entrepreneurs get frustrated when a client doesn't see the value of what they offer. But, unless you really believe in your results, you probably won't believe people will pay for them either.

Think about what most people want in life; they want to:

＊ Make (or save) more money

＊ Look good and feel better

＊ Find or maintain better relationships (including love)

＊ Protect themselves, their families, and their business from loss or harm

＊ Improve, upgrade, or transform their lives

＊ Impress other people

Now, don't freak out if your business doesn't immediately fit into an obvious category in the list above: you don't have to change your marketing completely. But you'll see how, by tapping into some of these desires, you can help your clients justify working with you, and it will immeasurably improve your offer. Here's my biggest tip:

Use Money Language in Your Marketing

You don't have to be a financial advisor, accountant, or bookkeeper to help people make more money, and you don't have to be richer than all of your clients to be able to tap into that desire. Does your business help people make or save money, even in an indirect way? You might not think so, but lots of different businesses can be tweaked to become more explicitly linked to money. See if you can answer this question:

'I help people ...., so they can make more money.'

You never have to put this on your sales pages if you don't want to, but if you can put any monetary figure on your results, you'll feel much better charging money for what you do because you can see a direct return on your customers' investment.

Here are a few examples:

❖ A graphic designer: 'I help people create amazing websites that attract more customers, which brings in more money.'

❖ An energy healer: 'I help entrepreneurs eliminate blocks and an energetic resistance to success, so they can be more confident and make more money.'

❖ A book coach: 'I help people write the best book they can, so they can reach more people and make more money.'

❖ A photographer: 'I help people show themselves, their products, and services in the best possible light, so their brand is magnetic, and they can make more money.'

❖ A stylist: 'I help women feel attractive and confident, so they can make more money in their businesses.'

You might feel adamant that your business is decidedly *not* about helping people make money. But does it save people time? Remember, 'time is money,' and for some customers, time is actually more valuable than money. How do you save people stress, time, or energy? Even if your business doesn't feel connected to money, you can still use money language to express the value of what you do. For example, *cost, spend, invest,* and *save*: 'I help you *save* time and energy, so you can *spend* more *priceless* time with your family.'

If your business is about the business of transformation, either in a wellness sense (health coach, weight loss), medical-based healing, or beauty, you can still use this language. Look at L'Oreal: they've used variations on 'I'm worth it' *for years*.

- ✤ Your health is *priceless*. You're *worth* spending *money* on.
- ✤ What is your health problem *costing* you right now?
- ✤ Health is *wealth*.
- ✤ Look and feel like a *million bucks*.
- ✤ *Invest* in your health, so you can *spend* more time with your loved ones.

You get the idea, right? What's the payoff for them working with you? What is it costing them not to work with you (in terms of time, energy, money, or peace of mind)?

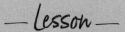

— Lesson —

Money language is powerful. It helps you and your customers see the value in what you do.

What if you help people with their relationships – anything from dating advice, marriage counseling, and parenting advice to matchmaking and networking services.

- ✤ *Save* your marriage.
- ✤ *Invest* in your child's self-esteem.
- ✤ Good relationships are *priceless*.

You can use this money language in subtle ways, or you can be explicit about how you can help people in any of these areas. This is especially important if you want to charge premium prices: your clients need to see the value in working with you.

EXERCISE: MONEY LANGUAGE

In your journal, or in a conversation with an entrepreneurial friend, answer these questions:

- How do I help clients make or save money?
- What is a priceless result I offer?
- What does it cost my clients not to work with me?
- How can I use money language in my marketing?

Make It Easy for People to Give You Money

If I see people I like or read an article about them that resonates with me, I often look for the next step to take with them, like buying their book or scheduling a private consultation. But most of the time, I find that there *is* no next step. There's no offer and no obvious way to give that person money, so I forget about it. Some entrepreneurs will do anything to avoid asking for the sale, including getting awkward at the very idea of money changing hands.

My best sales technique has been to say, 'I have this thing that could help. Here's how you can get this thing.' For example, 'I have a Money Bootcamp that could help you with your money blocks; here's where you sign up.' It's chill, it's straightforward, and it's non-sleazy.

Tell people what to do. I often use the words 'next step' in my marketing. I freely give information, and then I say, 'If you want to take this further, the next step is to sign up for my Money Bootcamp,' and I point them to the website. Easy. It's totally okay for you to make an offer, and it's okay for people to say no. But some people want and need exactly what you have, right now. Stop hoarding your talents. Help them give you money!

Business mentor Fabienne Fredrickson calls this 'sharing your brownies.' Imagine yourself hosting an informal dinner party for friends and spending the whole evening talking about the delicious brownies you just made. After dinner, you head off to the kitchen to get them but never return. Or you come back empty-handed and never mention them again. This awkward behavior is precisely what happens when entrepreneurs chicken out of asking for the sale. They build up all this anticipation for what they can do, and then they ghost! They don't follow through with the goods, and don't share their brownies! It's selfish.

Now, imagine that you do offer the brownies to your guests. Most people will *love* them. But, inevitably, there will be guests who are too full, on a diet, or just don't *like* brownies. Would you be offended (maybe) or cry (doubtful)? Would you be so disappointed that you refuse ever to hold a dinner party again? Probably not. Why? It's just brownies – some people like them, and some don't.

Someone once asked me, 'Denise, how do I buy your Money Bootcamp? Is there a special hidden password or something?' I thought, *What is she talking about? It's right there on my website!* But it wasn't. It was hidden behind pages of digital breadcrumbs. I thought it was obvious, but it required detective work to find. I was actively *hiding* my brownies! All the marketing techniques in the world aren't enough if you make your customers work to give you money. Make it an easy *yes* for them. Have an obvious 'Work with me' or 'Hire me' button on your website. At the bottom of every page, have a 'next step' call to action.

A comedian I follow has a plug for his book at the bottom of *every single blog post*. Eventually, I bought it because he kept reminding me! I see lots of entrepreneurs put out amazing content every week, but they don't give concrete solutions as a follow-up. They write thoughtful, useful newsletters and always provide value. Yet they ask *nothing* in return. If you don't ask, you don't get. Even toddlers know this. It's okay to say, 'Here's some free info, and if you want to take this further, here's how you can work with me.' Or 'Here's how you do XYZ, but if you want to outsource it, I can do it for you! Book here.' It honestly doesn't have to be more complicated than that.

Here are some examples:

- ❖ 'Here's your free weekly horoscope. If you want a more personalized, in-depth horoscope, you can buy it here.'

- ❖ 'Here's my DIY guide for making your own website in a weekend. If you'd rather have me do it for you, you can buy my website package here.'

- ❖ 'Here are three things I did to improve my own fertility. If you want even more tips on getting pregnant, you can buy my fertility book here.'

If you have a solution, why not just give it to people who need it, and just assume that people who want your help are willing to pay you for it. To those who write back and say, 'Oh, I was hoping you'd help me for free' (and they will), you can simply say, 'I can't help with that. Good luck with your search,' or just repeat the message, 'That's exactly what I do for my paying clients. Here's the link again.' If you have free or low-cost offerings, you could point people who are looking for free services to those.

You don't have to work with people for free. Offering them a different solution is okay. (There's advice on how to deal with persistent brain-pickers in Part III: Money.)

What to Offer When You're Starting Out

When in doubt about which products or services you should create first, offer your time. It can take months to write a book, create a course, or develop a product, but you can start making money right away through coaching, mentoring, consulting, training, or offering personal support.

When I started out as a life coach, all I had to sell was coaching sessions with me. I didn't have any books, courses, or events for people to buy. It was basic: an hour with me cost $75. I didn't even really specify what they'd get for that – I just promised an hour of 'coaching.' I didn't have a sales page or testimonials – just a payment link at the end of every blog post that basically went like this: *'Here's how to make a dream board. If you need help setting and achieving your goals, book a coaching session with me here.'*

In a world of carefully curated social media accounts, it's easy to forget that some people have a business at all! I often see 'empowering' posts with no indication whatsoever of what the poster actually does. Don't forget to tell people how you can help them. Making their day a bit brighter isn't enough (if there's nothing for them to buy, you've got a hobby, not a business). Remember this affirmation: *I serve, I deserve.*

It's okay to give to your audience, and it's okay to receive money in return. Making offers is just telling people how you can help them; it's the next logical step. And people will thank you for it!

Exercise: Providing Clarity for Your Customers

Go through your website, blog posts, and social media accounts (or get someone else to) and evaluate the following:

- Is it really clear how people can work with me?

- Am I giving them a next step?

- Am I making it really easy for people to give me money?

- Can I make it even *more* obvious?

How to Get People to Commit

I go to a local nail salon that *never* turns away a potential customer. Even if they're busy, they'll put your feet in warm water and give you a magazine. At that point, you're *committed*. Even if you sit there for 20 minutes, you feel like you're a customer, so you're not going to dry off your own feet and leave.

Contrast this to another salon I went to recently. I just needed a quick pedicure but they turned me away, even though the place was *totally empty*. They offered to fit me in, in three days' time; but if they had asked me what I wanted, I could have been out of there in 10 minutes.

As a family, the same thing often happens to us at restaurants. With young kids, you eat early and quickly; you're not lingering over dessert! But we get turned away all the time, even when the place is completely empty. We've since learned to say, 'We promise we'll be quick!' Or they could hand us a take-out menu and some free breadsticks while we wait. A bird in the hand is worth two in the bush!

I'm a *huge* fan of any restaurant that gives free food while I'm waiting, because I get hangry. Giving waiting customers a few nuts, olives, or chips and salsa (my favorite) is equivalent to putting my feet in warm water and bringing me a magazine. It inspires commitment, generates loyalty, and costs very little. I've walked out of restaurants after being ignored for ages, but had I been given free food, I would have happily waited for service. This has *huge* applications for any business. Do you see the theme? Micro-commitments! When you have available clients, ask them to commit to you in very small ways.

This is exactly what I did with 'mini-dates' when I conducted my internet dating research. What's the marketing equivalent of a mini-date? An offer to work with you. Most marketing gurus advocate giving a low-cost, low-commitment offer, like an e-book, a cheap course, or an inexpensive taster of your work, with the idea that this will be the 'gateway drug' to working with your further. You might have also heard this called a 'tripwire.' Basically, it's a tasty little snack that people can enjoy while they decide if they want to continue working with you.

The mini-date might be a free consultation to see if there's a fit on both sides – a casual 'try before you buy.' Your best customers are the ones who have already made a commitment to you, so give them the opportunity to buy *more*.

Don't be afraid to upsell. For example, one of my most popular freebies is my Manifesting Formula Workshop – there's no commitment other than providing an email address. At the end, I offer my Advanced Manifesting Course for $197, and if someone buys *that*, I casually suggest they join my Money Bootcamp; if they do that, I credit them for their Manifesting Course purchase. Not everyone takes me up on this offer, but enough people do to make it worthwhile. If you're interested in the statistics, the normal 1 percent of people buy the Manifesting Course, but a whopping 20 percent of those people upgrade to the Money Bootcamp at $2,000. Trust me: it's worth making the offer!

— *Lesson* —

Get people to commit to you – even in small ways.

Practice Your 'Closing' Technique

It's obvious to say, but you don't have a client until they've paid you some money.

When I was a teenager, I was a children's performer at a summer fair. Every day, I noticed that the most popular food stall was the corncob-on-a-stick. When the queue got out of control, the owners of the business did the most genius thing: they walked the length of it and collected everyone's money in advance. It was a pretty simple set-up: each corncob was $4, and you could pick any flavoring you wanted once you got to the counter. So, they collected the right amount of money and gave each person a ticket for pre-purchased corncobs. After a customer had paid, they were *not* going to leave that queue: they were committed.

I've had 'discovery' calls with potential suppliers who go round and round about their service until I finally say, 'Okay, how can we work together? Tell me the options.' I often have to sell myself to *them*! Then, even when they tell me the price, I have to say, 'Okay, how do you want me to pay? Do you take credit cards?' because they never ask! I'm very reluctant to get on the phone with anyone unless I'm interested in their service. Assume the same is true for your customers. Let them pay you money!

When I was offering coaching packages, I'd often give potential clients a free 'taster' session to see if there was a fit. At the end of the session, I'd pitch my services, and if a client was interested, I'd be ready to take a deposit over the phone to 'secure their spot,' otherwise they would inevitably chicken out or feel scared about taking action. Remember the corn stand? People who pay a deposit are *committed*.

Your fear of sales might come from watching movies like *Wall Street* or experiencing a pushy salesperson in real life. You might even have sat through an excruciating sales pitch and vowed never to be a sleazy salesperson *ever*. Well, it doesn't have to be that way. You're just making people an offer to work with you – not asking for a kidney!

If you practice your closing technique, you'll naturally find the best fit, won't sound like a robot, and won't forget to ask for the sale. With practice, you can be relaxed about asking for it without sounding vague or chickening out. Write your favorite closing technique on a Post-it and put it where you can see it while you're on sales calls. Here are some examples:

❖ Here are my three solutions, which one sounds best to you?

❖ How would you like to pay your deposit?

✦ Are you ready to book your first session?

✦ Seeing now what I offer, would you like my help?

Be prepared to get that money! Don't make people wait for the invoice – have payment options ready to go (especially over the phone), and don't chicken out of receiving that money, honey!

Sweeten the Deal

I love offering incentives for people to work with me, mainly because I know it works for me as a customer! I like an extra nudge to get off the fence, and if I get a sweet deal out of it, even better (especially if I was ready to buy anyway). For phone or webinar sales pitches, I often give a special price that's only valid for 24 hours or, if I'm selling on stage, it's for 'today only.' Your sales incentive could be a limited-time discount or an added bonus that's valid only for the first few customers. (There are some extra tips on incentives in Part III: Money.)

Again, this doesn't have to be pushy or salesy. There's a way to do it that's open, transparent, and kind. I openly tell customers that the reason I offer an incentive is that I know some people need a nudge to do something they want to anyway. And I remind them that, if they sign up later, they'll just have to pay full price, so no big deal either way. I'm giving them an option and a choice to take it. I've seen this done in sleazy ways, like, *'Run to the back of the room now and sign up or you're a loser!'* but it's all in the delivery. Make it a reward, rather than a penalty.

— *Lesson* —

**People won't have an opportunity to
work with you unless you ask.**

Overcoming the Fear of Rejection

Let's reframe 'selling' into 'service.' You're not taking people's money: you're making a fair exchange. They're investing in themselves, and you're providing a valuable service in return.

The idea of hearing no might be terrifying to you, but you're going to hear it a lot more than you'll hear yes. Remember the 1 percent conversion rule. If you focus on the fact that 99 percent of people will say no, you might never get started, so you have to focus on the *yesses*. Sometimes no means a 'not now.' Sometimes what you're offering isn't a good fit for a prospective client (or you). Sometimes customers would genuinely work with you if they had the money. It's tough when you know they need you, but their inability to afford you is honestly none of your business. Move on to the next person you can help.

You might even have had old clients stop working with you. It will happen, and you'll want to grab their ankles as they walk away and scream: *Why are you leaving meeeeeeee?'* But the best thing for you (and your dignity) is to let them go. It's not personal. There are many reasons why someone says no (that have nothing to do with your talent), for example:

❀ They don't need what you're offering right now.

❀ They are *shocked, disappointed,* and even *angry* that you're selling them something. (These people are not your customers.)

❀ They're just not that into you or your style of doing business. (These people are not your customers.)

❀ They don't have the money (right now).

❀ They think they can do it themselves.

❀ They don't understand what it takes to get the results you offer.

Either way, it's none of your business. It's okay for someone to say no, and there are plenty more fish in the sea. Not everyone has to be your client. Here's the truth: if you can't handle even the tiniest bit of rejection, you're going to struggle in business. If you're too scared to ask for the sale because people might say no (and they will), then you won't have the opportunity to serve the people who *want* to work with you.

That's not to say rejection is fun. I'm not like, 'Bye, bitch!' every time someone says no. I've never been rude back or said: 'Well, you're doomed to fail, then.' I try to be gracious about it. It's not personal and I just move on. Sometimes those 'no' clients are ready to work with you in the future, so don't burn those bridges. Your business won't be successful in a day. Your community won't be built in a week. It's going to take time, so show up and be consistent. Every no will get you closer to *yes*.

The original *Chicken Soup for the Soul* book was rejected 144 times; today, that series has sold more than 100 million books. The novel *The Help* received 60 rejections, but eventually it was on the *New York Times* bestseller list for more than 100 weeks and was made into a movie that received more than 40 awards.[1] Author Kathryn Stockett says '... letter number 61 was the one that accepted me. What if I had given up at 15? Or 40? Or even 60?'[2]

I've been rejected so many times on the path to a million-dollar business. But I don't focus on that. Rejection is just inevitable, and I'm not willing to let it stand in the way of my dream life. Neither should you.

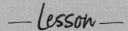

— *Lesson* —

If you never ask, the answer is always no.

How to Reject 'Wrong Fit' Clients

At some point during the sales process, you'll realize that you can't, don't want to, or *shouldn't* work with some potential clients. Maybe you're seeing red flags about their temperament; perhaps they're at the wrong stage of life and business for your expertise, or they see you as a silver-bullet solution to their problems. Pretty much every entrepreneur I know has taken clients when they should have known better, but you'll learn that through trial and error (and it's a rite of passage anyway!)

Some businesses even use rejection in their marketing, like the canned seafood brand John West. Their slogan 'It's what John West rejects that makes John West the best' recently got changed to a simple 'It's a No from John West.' Are you exclusive? Do people have to jump through hoops to work with you? Make that really clear in your marketing – not only to pre-screen clients but to get them excited about working with you.

I once asked my friend for a recommendation for an accountant, and before she gave me a name, she said, 'He doesn't work with *everyone*. He only works with people he really believes in.' I was nervous and went into the introductory meeting trying to sell myself to *him!* Like, 'Please sir, can I give you some money?'

You'll start to realize who you can and can't help, and it's okay to say no. You're not rejecting abundance from the universe – you're being really smart and discerning. No amount of money is worth accepting for a situation you know is going to cause you stress. Over time, you'll get better at pre-screening your potential clients, but some will slip through your net, so you have to be able to skillfully say no to them. How? Make it about *you*, not *them*, but saying:

- ✦ That's not my area of expertise.

- ✦ I don't think I'm the best person for you.

- ✦ I'd love to help, but I can recommend someone who's a better fit.

- ✦ I'm booked out right now (white lies are okay sometimes).

The most gracious way I've handled it is to say, 'Look, I'd gladly take your money, but from my experience with this particular situation, I know I'm not the best person to help you. It just won't be a good use of your investment.' Then I recommend a different solution – in the form of a book, resource, course, or another provider who's a better fit.

Ignore your gut at your peril. I've had friends who ignored the signs because they needed the money and ended up in ligation with disgruntled clients, turned off other customers (in retreat or group coaching settings), or just ended up in a miserable experience all round. *Listen to your gut!*

— *Lesson* —

You don't have to work with everyone.

How to Prevent Buyer's Remorse

Have you ever had a client who was enthusiastic to work with you and then ghosted when you sent an invoice? Or worse, paid and then, days later, asked for a refund? Yeah, me too. It sucks, but you can avoid it with a few more micro-commitments post-purchase.

Your after-sales service is incredibly important. One of my pet peeves is when you buy something online and then hear nothing. You feel like the sale was the most important thing, and now you're an actual paying client, you're at the bottom of their priority list. Remember, getting the sale is half the battle – now you have to deliver the goods to ensure a happy customer!

Don't make people guess or wonder what happens next. On your online thank-you pages, tell them what to do next in really simple language. I usually make a simple video, saying something like, 'Thanks for your purchase. Here's *exactly* what to do next.' If you need people to fill in a form or schedule time with you, make it incredibly obvious. I've even seen screenshots of what the email the customer will get looks like, and a reminder to check their spam folder. Show your customer service email address, so they know how and where to get help.

Embrace the keyless life philosophy and set up autoresponders and automated receipts, so you don't have to do any of this manually. Use an online scheduling system, so you don't have to chase people down to find a mutually convenient time to talk. Make your life and theirs as easy as possible. Good follow-up helps clients avoid buyer's remorse and makes them feel committed. Yes, they just gave you their money, but you want them to feel safe and secure about it, even after clicking the 'Buy now' button. You don't want them to worry whether they've made the wrong decision. Trust me: that's when you'll get refund requests, even from people who literally *just* bought from you.

On my Money Bootcamp thank-you page, I have a little video of current members giving advice about how to get the most out of the course, and even about how nervous they were to join at first. This assures new members that they've made the right decision. I also provide the link to the member's group right away. Joining a group and introducing themselves is a micro-commitment that's a lot easier than diving straight into a course. We've done the research, and members who join the group are way less likely to ask for a refund, especially if they had tech problems getting in or their introductory email went into spam (things that make them think they made the wrong decision).

Another way to delight your clients and inspire loyalty is to add unexpected surprises after they buy. For example, you could send them some of your favorite resources or tools to help them – something they can access right away (like a metaphorical free chips and salsa) that will solidify their commitment to working with you.

Now, a *huge* mistake that entrepreneurs make is over-delivering in ways that cause stress, cost money, and lead to unnecessary waste.

There's nothing wrong with being generous to your clients, but do it appropriately, and don't create extra work for yourself unless it's in line with what you're offering. For example, my web designer, Ellissa Jayne, sent me a cinema gift card when I signed with her and flowers when we wrapped up the new site. It wasn't a cheap project – it was a significant investment in my website – and Ellissa treated me like a VIP. That's appropriate.

Doing it for someone who has bought a cheap course or e-book? No: that's not sustainable for your business. Instead of mailing presents to every single client, consider freebies that don't cost you much, but are valuable to them. For example, my Money Bootcamp students get free access to many of my other courses and programs, which don't 'cost' me anything and are completely automated to deliver. Keep physical gifts to a minimum and save the high-end items for your high-end clients.

EXERCISE: RETHINKING CLIENT CARE

Go through your after-sale process and evaluate:

- Do my clients know *exactly* what to do after they purchase?
- What else can I put on my 'thank-you' page?
- What processes can I automate post-sale?
- What bonuses can I offer to surprise and delight my customers?

Your Simple Marketing Plan

Remember, marketing boils down to two things: share and make offers. Your marketing plan doesn't have to be complicated. *Something* is better than nothing, and you'll be surprised by how much progress you can make, even if you half-ass it. Keep it simple, tweak as you go, but above all, take action!

Below, I've compiled all the marketing questions in this section into a simple marketing plan that you can customize, and I've also included my own marketing plan. (You can download both at Chillpreneur.com/Bonus.) You don't have to answer every question. Choose the ones that will move your business forward, and take action. If you improve just one thing a month, it will make a huge difference in your business.

The 1 Percent Conversion Rule

Remember, for a mass-market campaign, your results will be 1 to 2 percent. If you're selling from the stage, it could be five to 15 percent, and if you're selling over the phone, it could be 25 to 75 percent.

✦ How many clients could I realistically handle right now (considering time, energy, systems, and customer service)?

✦ To hit my sales targets, how many potential customers do I need to reach?

Show Up, Be Seen and Be Heard

✦ What free content do I want to create?

✦ What incentives do I have for people to join my email list or subscribe to my updates on social media?

✦ What Hairy Toes Strategy would work best for my audience?

✦ Which topics are in scope and out of scope for my business?

✦ Can I stop some of my marketing efforts? If so, which ones?

✦ Which marketing medium works best for me?

✦ How often do I want to contact my audience?

✦ Which marketing tasks could I batch?

Make Offers

◈ What do my customers really want? What's their biggest desire?

◈ How can I bring money language into my marketing?

◈ What micro-commitments would work for my audience?

◈ Am I being clear about the benefits of working with me?

◈ What red flags should I look out for in potential clients?

◈ How could I be clearer in asking for a sale?

◈ How can I avoid buyer's remorse?

 **The Big Idea**

If you remember nothing else from Part IV of the book, remember this: *Marketing is simply manifesting the clients you need to create a successful business!*

Your Mission

'My mission, should I choose to accept it, is to find peace with exactly who and what I am. To take pride in my thoughts, my appearance, my talents, my flaws and to stop this incessant worrying that I can't be loved as I am.'

ANAÏS NIN

In this last section, we're going to talk about your mission and legacy. You might think we'd start here and work our way back to designing your business around it, but I find that, for most entrepreneurs, mission evolves over time.

After all, when you start your business, you're often in survival mode, and your biggest mission might be to quit your job (as it was for me), be able to support yourself in your new business, or buy something specific like a new house or car. And that's okay! Once you get past survival mode, it's time for 'sur-thrival.' How can you use business as a vehicle to live your passion, develop your calling, give back, build a legacy, and change the world?

You may feel it's your destiny to be rich, successful, or influential in some way. You feel it in your bones, and you know it will happen eventually, even on the days when you're second-guessing yourself. You might also have felt that you've been put on this planet, at this exact moment, to help people. Maybe you're actually scared of the potential inside you and judge yourself for being grandiose or self-important. *Will I ever be happy with a normal life?* you might wonder. *Why am I compelled to do things that are so scary?*

Some days are easy: creativity flows into your life's work; you have clients who tell you that you're changing their lives; your bank account is healthy; and you feel like you're living your purpose. Other days, you wonder: if this is my destiny, why is it so freaking *hard*? Why do I feel such resistance and fear? The unsexy secret is that we have to go on a journey and encounter practical realities along the way. If it were easy, everyone would do it. But they don't. In fact, sometimes I meet people from my 'old life' who have heard third-hand about my financial success and say, 'Oh, maybe I should start a blog, too.' I smile to myself, and think, *Cool: do that!* But I know most of them won't.

When you find your calling, you don't suddenly get a parade in your honor. It's a slower process of uncovering, refining, tweaking, evolving, and changing. Your mission will probably change over time as you grow and evolve. Your destiny is heading toward you, inevitably but slowly. By keeping your dream alive and taking at least one baby step toward it every day, you'll bring it so much closer.

I know that my mission is to help a lot of women, but I'm also okay being a normal person with ups and downs. I'm sure that some years I'm going to exceed my goals and others will be average. I'm not beating myself up to be the best all the time, and neither should you. Remember, there's no need to be Wonder Woman.

What Will Your Legacy Be?

After Oprah returned from South Africa, where she visited her newly created girl's leadership school, she told the late writer and activist

Maya Angelou, 'This school will be my greatest legacy. It will make such a profound difference. It will change the trajectory of the girls' lives. It will impact generations to come.'

Maya interrupted Oprah: 'You have no idea what your legacy will be!' she said. 'Your legacy is every life you touch! It's every person who ever watched your show and felt something. Was moved to do something. Go back to school, leave an abusive marriage, stop hitting their kids, no longer remain silent, not be a victim. It's not one thing – it's *everything!*'[1]

So, let me tell you: you have no idea what your legacy will be, so don't stress too much about it right now. You don't need to know all the details before you start. You have no idea how many people will be touched by your business, your leadership example, your messages, and the sheer audacity of showing up. Maybe your only mission is to be yourself and contribute one tiny puzzle piece to creating heaven on Earth. You don't have to be a missionary *or* a millionaire to do that. *You* are enough. Why else did you agree to come to the planet at this time, if not to play a part?

To end this book, I want to channel Oprah and give you some 'What I know for sure' takeaways for you and your business.

Build Philanthropy into Your Business, Your Way

> *'Abundance isn't just about money. It's about being able to live in the overflow, where you've filled yourself up so much, that you have so much to give.'*
> DR. EZZIE SPENCER

I've mentioned many times in this book that getting to a place where you can charge well for what you do puts you in a powerful position to help others. But that doesn't mean confusing running a business with becoming a charity. It's okay to embrace 'sustainable philanthropy.' It's okay to make sure that your bills and needs are taken care of before you give to others. You don't have to give away all your profits to 'deserve' success.

It's also okay to start where you are right now. Start with the idea of yourself as a wealthy philanthropist and act accordingly with what you have available. You might decide to give away 10 percent of your profits to charity or choose to build in a 'buy one, donate one' model, like Toms Shoes, Bombas socks, or Warby Parker glasses (companies that donate a product to someone in need for every one that's purchased).

It's also okay to make money and give in other ways. Sometimes you have money to give, and other times you just have time. Sometimes all you can do is sign a petition, and other times you can sponsor others to be activists. Sometimes you have wisdom or a kind word to share. Other times you can be a kind boss, hire other women, or use ethical suppliers. You don't have to give in any particular way.

Be a Beacon for Others

> *'you are here for a reason... you are*
> *here to shine your light.'*
>
> KAREN GUNTON

In the early days of my business, each time one of my business buddies or people on a business forum posted about their success, it made my heart leap. I'd say to Mark, 'Come and look at this. My friend just made *5,000 dollars* in one day!' I was celebrating, but I was also saying, 'Wow, she did it, and she's not that different from me. Maybe I can too?'

One of the most generous things you can do for your community (and that includes your family, friends, business network, clients and peers) is to share your successes and your failures. Be human, and you'll be surprised at how many people are inspired by you. Exactly as you are.

My mission is to help women become financially independent and either inspire or empower other women to do the same. Together we're normalizing money, wealth, and success for other women.

Business Serves Your Life, Not The Other Way Around

'I do not think I am successful just because I have money. I'm successful because I love who I am and I have no regrets, and I'm successful because I have a great heart and I have compassion and I care and I would be happy with or without money.'

SUZE ORMAN

My work is my life. But in addition to being my calling and mission, my business is a job, which means I can take a day off now and then, and you can too!

In his book *The War Of Art*, Steven Pressfield says that 'Madonna does not identify with "Madonna." Madonna employs "Madonna."' I feel the same about 'Lucky Bitch Denise.' She works for me: the real Denise who makes mistakes, farts out loud, and is sometimes not very nice to her husband. What if you treated the public persona you've created as your employee? Would you be kinder? Less critical? Take more days off?

It's okay to create a business vehicle that supports your life, not one you have to give your life up to support. You can hold your legacy lightly. It doesn't have to weigh down on you and be super-serious.

It's Not About the Money (But the Money Is Really Nice)

'Money is power, money is freedom, money is confidence, money is "Creepy boss, take your hand off of my leg." Money is "I'm starting my dream business."'

SALLIE KRAWCHECK

When I was starting out, I asked my mentor Sandy Forster, author of *How to Be Wildly Wealthy Fast*, when she first realized she was rich. She said she was buying a blender and realized she could choose any one she wanted. She literally burst into tears in the department store. I have that moment every time I'm food shopping and realize that I can choose the expensive tomatoes. That's what I want for you, too. For you to be, do, and have everything on your dream board *and* be able to have the peace of mind that comes with being able to choose what you want on a daily basis, regardless of the cost.

It's okay to be motivated by the money as much as the mission. Being rich is really nice. I love being rich. Beyond being able to build my dream home, buy new cars and travel First Class with my family, I love that I've completely paid back my student loans and years of government support through the taxes I've paid back into the system.

I love hiring other women, buying from other women, spending money on supporting local economies, being able to support my family financially, and having more than enough to share around. There's nothing better than not having to rely on others for your support. It's one of the best things a woman can do and it sets an example to the younger generation.

There's Time for Your Life to Unfold

> *'You are the designer of your destiny;*
> *you are the author of your story.'*
> LISA NICHOLS

Chill out. You don't have to write all the books you want to write this year, you don't have to go to all the conferences right away, and you don't have to reserve all the domain names yet. There's time. Be discerning. Some things are more urgent than others and, if you're in business for the long haul, you have to respect the seasons of your life. I'm in my child-raising season right now, and that means I can't do *everything* right now. I'm (mostly) okay with that.

If you want to create a real legacy, your journey has to be sustainable. Being an entrepreneur is like always having an urgent assignment due. You feel guilty if you're not working on your latest project, and there's never a time when you feel 'done.' The next assignment is always due, so you have to pace yourself.

Your mission and legacy might not be apparent yet, but there's time to figure it out. As my friend Amber McCue says, 'Don't try and boil the ocean.' It's okay to focus on your corner of the entrepreneurial world and not put pressure on yourself. It's okay to park some dreams for 'one day.'

There's time.

Don't Wait Too Long

> *'You don't have to get it right, you just have to get it going.'*
> BARBARA CORCORAN

Although there's time for life to unfold, you can't wait until everything's perfect before you start! On some days, half-assed baby steps will be enough. Other days you'll have to take big, bold action. The truth is that nobody is really waiting for you to be ready, and the timing will never be perfect. There's always another Mercury retrograde around the corner, there are always other more pressing projects, and there's never going to be enough time.

Having a big dream or a sense of destiny is only half the equation. You have to put yourself in the right place to do the work. You can't just sit around and dream. You'll need to take courses, get coaching, pay taxes, do admin work. You can't do it all yourself, and most importantly, you don't have to. Keep one eye on your Big Dream in the future and one eye on what needs to happen *today*. Your dream just has to be slightly bigger and more exciting than your fear. That will give you the courage to act in all sorts of ways that most people won't, including taking risks that scare you.

Demanding that your destiny unfold without taking intentional action is delusional. Some days are easier than others, and you'll feel like the heavens are smiling down on you. Other days you'll just want to give up. That's understandable. But...

Don't Wait for Perfection

*'The big break is the moment you decide
to take your dream seriously.'*

ALEXANDRA FRANZEN

This book is a perfect example of choosing myself. I self-published my first two books because I had zero list, zero marketing platform, and zero appeal to a mainstream publisher. My first book wasn't that great. Nobody liked the title, *Lucky Bitch*, but I'd asked the universe for a 'bestselling book idea' and got that one in the shower. The first few versions had lots of typos and amateur covers. But I chose myself. I had a message and luckily, thanks to self-publishing, I had a platform through which I could share it. I didn't ask for permission to become an author.

Publishing with Hay House was a long-held dream, but I didn't sit and wait for them to call. I chose myself. I built my subscriber list (starting with plenty of no-show webinars and small local events), pitched myself on podcasts, and showed up, even when I felt like an unworthy fraud. I didn't ask anyone to choose me as a speaker because I created my own events, even when there were just four people in the room. I applied for industry awards and didn't wait to be 'chosen' as an award winner.

There are many paths to success. Do you need to get up at 4 a.m. every day to be rich? Do you need a tidy desk? No. Get up when you want to, be as messy as you like. Success isn't absolute. Success doesn't have a weight or height limit. Success looks like *you*. If you have a dream, be patient and *do the work*. It's up to you. Don't wait for someone to choose you, because you might be waiting a long time, and most people lose interest if things don't manifest instantly. I've been working on this goal for years. Patience is not always my virtue, but I've held firm in keeping the dream alive because, along the way, I've decided that I'm enough.

Show up, show up, show up.

Be the Keeper of the Flame

> *'I had to go out in the world and become*
> *strong, to discover my mission in life.'*
>
> TINA TURNER

For the longest time, I was frustrated that Mark couldn't see my vision as clearly as I could. I was angry that he wouldn't quit his job as cavalierly as I did to join the world of entrepreneurship. I didn't understand why he was content with our life the way it was: with climbing the corporate ladder at his company, and with keeping our dreams 'realistic.'

Then I realized that it was up to me. It was *my* job to keep the vision alive. It was up to *me* to dream it and make it happen for our family. I had the inner strength and the capability – I just had to believe in myself. Rather than being scary, that realization was empowering. I decided to stop blaming Mark for his 'lack of vision' and set our GPS onto a new path instead.

After all, if it's meant to be, it's up to me.

Would you let one hater comment or a one-star review snuff out your dream? No. You are stronger than that. I know you're tired and you've been working hard, but don't give up now. Let the fire of your dream fuel you to the next stage. The person that you think you'll become one day? You're already that person. Why would you be given a vision and not be given the ability to make it come true? Keep the flame of your vision alive and use it as a beacon that will help you find your way there.

Honor Your Grandmother

> *'We are such stuff as our grandmothers'*
> *dreams were made on.'*
>
> D.H. LAWRENCE

Think of your lineage – it's full of women; some were strong, some were broken, some were trailblazers, and some were downtrodden. Every single one of them has led you to this point. Who are you to deny their legacy now, when you can change things for the future and create a new legacy?

My ancestors undoubtedly faced way tougher situations than having to have awkward money conversations while sitting in yoga pants. If I connect to them now, I can feel centuries of oppression, poverty, famine, and certainly, for the women, lack of opportunity and freedom. I have that freedom now, so how can I not use it?

My Nan, Judy Thomas, took in sewing for extra money (and apparently once spilled a cup of tea on a wedding dress that she then had to unpick and start over with), and she would be amazed at how many options women have to make their own money in this golden age. We once went on a road trip together and the whole way, we listened to some old white dude talking about success. After four hours, she turned to me and said, 'You could do this.' I wish she was here to see my success. I'm sure she'd be proud – not of the trappings, but of the fact that I earn my own money.

> *'I think the girl who is able to earn her own living and pay*
> *her own way should be as happy as anybody on earth.*
> *The sense of independence and security is very sweet.'*
>
> SUSAN B. ANTHONY

Think back to all the women you're descended from. Some might have become entrepreneurs out of necessity. Some were stuck in unsatisfying marriages because they were completely dependent on their husband and had no 'running away money.' Some put up with relentless sexual harassment at work because they had mouths to feed. Many died with books unpublished, ideas unmanifested, and burning ambitions unrealized.

Our grandmothers would be astounded by the world we live in today. We can take an idea and, with nothing more than our phones and this magical thing called the internet, be selling something to the whole world by the weekend! We can help/coach/teach/counsel someone for an hour online and get paid for it! With a few clicks of a button, we can design something, have it made, and ship it without needing our own factory. What? It's *crazy*!

What if you could go back in time and ask all the women whose lives and sacrifices led you here, 'What do you want for me?' I'm sure they'd want you to have independence, the freedom to live your dreams, and to be happy. Let's not waste this opportunity. Be brave enough to create financial independence, grow a vehicle for your freedom, and give yourself permission to take this journey. We're the ones who can realize the dreams of our mothers and grandmothers.

A Final Message

> *'There are people less qualified than you doing*
> *the things you want to do simply because they*
> *decided to believe in themselves. Period.'*
>
> UNKNOWN

I hope you'll join me in this new revolution of women who are rising up, breaking all the rules about what it means to be successful, and using entrepreneurship and money as a tool for good in the world.

This is the *best* time to be a woman and an entrepreneur. We owe it to our ancestors, our sisters, and our children to step up. Welcome to the world of the Chillpreneur. Remember, it doesn't need to be that hard.

Chill. There's time.

Find the path of least resistance.

Take baby steps toward realizing your vision.

You are enough.

It's your time.

Why not you?

xx *Denise*

P.S. Before you go, I've a few favors to ask: if you liked this book, please share with your business bestie. Let's grow and support each other to make more money. Please post a picture of yourself reading this book: it honestly makes my day to see women from all around the world working on their business and money mindset. I'm on Instagram at @denisedt; tag your picture #chillpreneur.

Don't forget to register for your book bonuses at Chillpreneur. com/Bonus. You'll also then be on my newsletter, so we can keep in touch!

References

Chapter 1: Playing the Game of Business

1. Katha Pollitt, 'Hers; The Smurfette Principle': www.nytimes. com/1991/04/07/magazine/hers-the-smurfette-principle.html

2. Kimberley Jones, 'What is the Witch Wound?': www.kimberleyjones .com/witch-wound/#sthash.KuH71lym.dpbs

3. ibid.

4. Ewen Callaway, 'Fearful Memories Passed Down to Mice Descendants': www.scientificamerican.com/article/fearful-memories-passed-down

5. Natalie Ann Taggart, 'Healing the Witch Wound': www.huffingtonpost.com/entry/healing-the-witch-wound_us_5a259f77e4b05072e8b56b70

6. ibid.

7. Seren Bertrand, 'Wound of the Witches': www.thefountainoflife.org /wound-of-the-witches

8. Sheryl Sandberg, *Lean In: Women, Work, and the Will to Lead*; p.28; Knopf, 2013.

9. Valerie Young, *The Secret Thoughts of Successful Women: Why Capable People Suffer from the Impostor Syndrome and How to Thrive in Spite of It*, p.40; Crown Business, 2011.

Chapter 2: Beliefs that Can Limit Your Success in Business

1. Marianne Schnall, 'The Rising Activism in Women's Philanthropy': www.forbes.com/sites/marianneschnall/2018/02/02/the-rising-activism-in-womens-philanthropy/#1035b58e44a9

Chapter 3: Millionaire Mindset Lessons

1. Esther Hicks, Jerry Hicks, *The Astonishing Power of Emotions: Let Your Feelings Be Your Guide*, p.44; Hay House, 2008.
2. Gary Chapman, *The Five Love Languages: How to Express Heartfelt Commitment to Your Mate*, Northfield Publishing, 1995.
3. Dictionary.com
4. Thomas J. Stanley, William D. Danko, *The Millionaire Next Door: The Surprising Secrets of America's Wealthy*, p.1; Taylor Trade Publishing, 2010.

Chapter 5: Are You Killing the Golden Goose?

1. Paul F. Boller Jr., *Hollywood Anecdotes*, p.262; Ballantine Books, 1988.
2. Ruthanne Reid, 'How to kill your "darlings" and survive the process': https://thewritepractice.com/kill-your-darlings
3. Sarah Wilson, 'A long letter about my business': www.sarahwilson.com/2018/02/long-letter-business

Chapter 7: Five Essentials for a Chillpreneur Business

1. www.investopedia.com/terms/p/passiveincome.asp
2. Amber McCue, 'My cloning secret': https://niceops.com/get-efficient-prioritization-matrix

Chapter 8: Big Pricing Mistakes

1. Carly Findlay, 'Why I won't provide disability advice for free': http://carlyfindlay.com.au/2014/11/09/why-i-wont-provide-disability-advice-for-free
2. ibid.
3. Andrew Pollack, 'Drug Goes From $13.50 a Tablet to $750, Overnight': www.nytimes.com/2015/09/21/business/a-huge-overnight-increase-in-a-drugs-price-raises-protests.html

Chapter 11: The 1 Percent Conversion Rule

1. ABC 10 News, 'Customers upset with Passion Planner delays': www.youtube.com/watch?v=kIzd8UWXSqw

Chapter 12: Cat Charming and Internet Dating

1. www.kathrynhocking.com

Chapter 13: Show Up, Be Seen, and Be Heard

1. Kruse Control Inc: 'The Rule of 7': www.krusecontrolinc.com/rule-of-7-how-social-media-crushes-old-school-marketing

2. https://www.iconundies.com

Chapter 14: Make Offers, Make Money

1. https://en.wikipedia.org/wiki/List_of_accolades_received_by_The_Help_(film)

2. Susan Gabriel, 'The Help Turned Down 60 Times': www.susangabriel.com/writers-and-writing/kathryn-stockett

Your Mission

1. Oprah.com, 'What Oprah Knows for Sure About Being a Supportive Friend': www.oprah.com/inspiration/what-oprah-knows-for-sure-about-being-a-supportive-friend

ABOUT THE AUTHOR

Denise Duffield-Thomas is a lazy self-made millionaire and unbusy mother of three children. Her best-selling books give a fresh and funny road map to creating an outrageously successful life and business.

As a money mindset mentor, Denise helps women release their fear of money, set premium prices for their services, and take back control over their finances.

She is an award-winning speaker, author, and entrepreneur who helps women transform their Economy-Class mindset into a First-Class life.

Denise lives with her family by the beach in sunny Australia. Find her at www.DeniseDT.com

 DeniseDT

 DeniseDT

 DeniseDT

www.DeniseDT.com